THE GERMAN INFANTRYMAN ON THE EASTERN FRONT

SIMON FORTY &
RICHARD CHARLTON-TAYLOR

CASEMATE | ILLUSTRATED

brau

CIS0037

Print Edition: ISBN 978-1-63624-361-0
Digital Edition: ISBN 978-1-63624-362-7

Design by Eleanor Forty-Robbins
Printed and bound in the Czech Republic by FINIDR s.r.o.

CASEMATE PUBLISHERS (US)
Telephone (610) 853-9131
Fax (610) 853-9146
Email: casemate@casematepublishers.com
www.casematepublishers.com

CASEMATE PUBLISHERS (UK)
Telephone (0)1226 734350
Email: casemate-uk@casematepublishers.co.uk
www.casematepublishers.co.uk

Acknowledgements: All photos credited on the captions. The authors thank all those who have contributed, in particular Ruth Sheppard, Chris Cocks, and Lizzy Hammond for constructive assistance in squeezing a quart into a pint pot, Eleanor Forty-Robbins (design) and Mark Franklin (artwork). Reenactment photographs are of the 304th Panzergrenadier Reenactment Group. If we've omitted any accreditation, please let us know through the publisher.

Page 1: Fritz Brauner's watercolor from *Soldaten in Eis und Schnee* (*Soldiers in Ice and Snow*) shows a 3.7cm Pak 36 antitank gun position. *RCT*

This page: Map shows position of the German advance on December 6, 1941. *Library of Congress (LoC)*

Right: The German infantryman of 1941 was part of an army used to winning, and initially the attack on the Soviet Union proved devastating. However, the army's main strength was in its soldiers—particularly the excellent, well-trained junior officers and NCOs who handled the close fighting. As attrition took its toll, so the *Ostheer*—the German Army in the east—lost skills and leadership it could never replace. *Narodowe Archiwum Cyfrowe/Polish National Archives (NAC)*

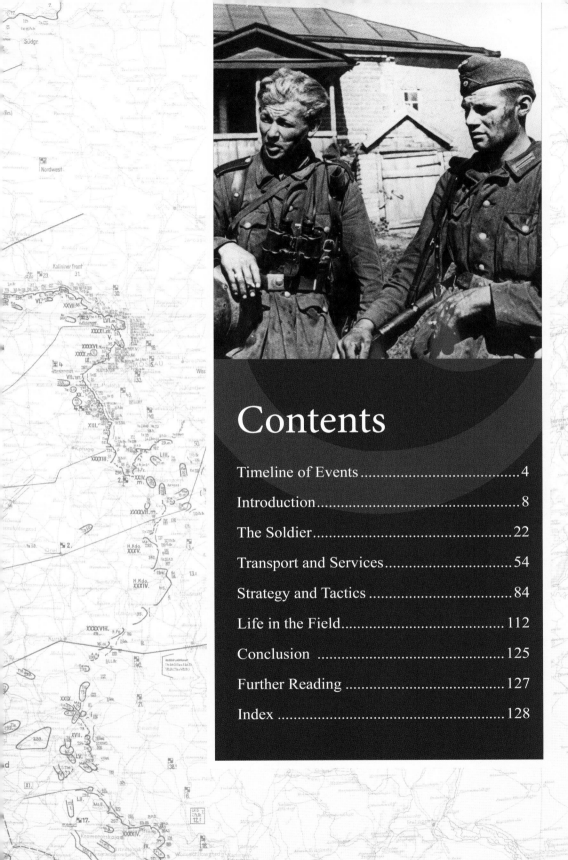

Contents

| Timeline of Events

June 22, 1941: *Barbarossa* launched—the Axis invasion of the Soviet Union.

June 25, 1941: Continuation War between Finland and USSR begins.

July 10–September 10, 1941: Battle of Smolensk; Soviet 16th and 20th Armies encircled.

August 8–September 19, 1941: Battle of Kiev; Soviet Southwestern Front encircled.

September 8, 1941–January 18, 1944: The siege of Leningrad lasts 872 days.

October 24, 1941: German advance on Moscow begins.

December 5, 1941: Soviet counteroffensive begins.

October 30, 1941–July 4, 1942: Siege of Sevastopol.

December 25, 1941–May 19, 1942: Soviet Kerch–Feodosia amphibious operation to break the siege of Sevastopol; *Unternehmen Trappenjagd* (Bustard Hunt) eventually clears the peninsula.

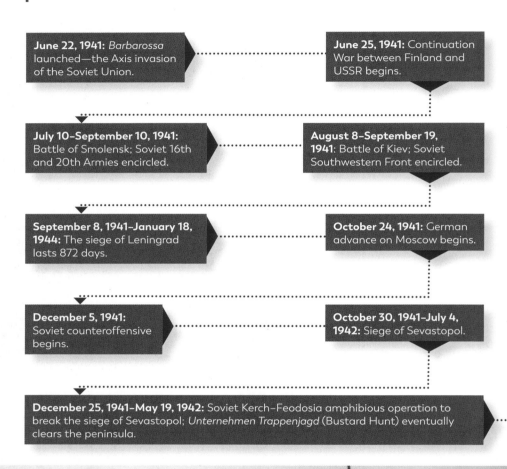

There comes a point when even tracked vehicles succumb to the mud. The SdKfz 10 was the smallest of the German halftrack prime movers (other than the Kettenkrad) and was used to tow light guns like this Pak 40. There were never enough halftracks: by 1943 only 10 percent of the panzergrenadier battalions used them, the rest used trucks. *RCT*

Fuel up when the opportunity arises. On the road is a 4x4 Horch 1A and at the left a BMW Kfz4 4x4 mounting twin MG 34s. *RCT*

February 8–May 20, 1942: Demyansk pocket withstands Soviet attacks.

May 12–30, 1942: Second battle of Kharkov; Soviet spring offensive ends with annihilation.

June 28, 1942: *Fall Blau* (Case Blue); the Axis summer offensive starts.

August 23, 1942: Battle of Stalingrad begins.

November 19, 1942: Soviet Operation *Uranus* begins encirclement of German 6. Armee at Stalingrad.

February 2, 1943: Paulus surrenders 6. Armee to the Soviets; the long retreat begins.

February 1943: Kharkov falls to the Soviets but Manstein's counterattack traps the overextended Red Army forces.

March 1–22, 1943: German 9. Armee evacuates Rzhev salient.

July 5–16, 1943: Battle of Kursk ends in German defeat and major withdrawal.

A sketch by Ernst Eigener. *RCT*

August 4–23, 1943: Fourth battle of Kharkov sees the city fall to the Soviets.

September–November 1943: Battle of the Dnieper; Germans retreat across the river but Soviets establish bridgeheads.

February 3–17, 1944: The Korosun pocket forms; eight German divisions are destroyed.

March 8, 1944: Führer Order No. 11 identifies 29 locations to serve as *Festungen* (fortresses).

June 10–19, 1944: Soviets break through the Mannerheim Line; Gulf of Finland now open to the Red Baltic Fleet

June 22, 1944: Soviet Operation *Bagration* heralds the destruction of Heeresgruppe Mitte and the Soviet advance to the Vistula.

July–August 1944: The Lvov–Sandomierz offensive destroys Heeresgruppe Süd.

August 7, 1944: *Bagration* closes, having advanced 450 miles.

August 20–29, 1944: German 6. Armee destroyed in Romania; the Romanians switch sides.

August 26, 1944: Bulgaria withdraws from Axis and Soviets invade on September 8.

German troops examine an SVT-40. Over 1.5 million were produced, but production was slowed by the German invasion. The Mosin-Nagant rifle and PPSh-41 SMG were preferred for ease of manufacture and use. *NAC*

September 14–November 24, 1944: Baltic offensive sees Estonia and Lithuania fall to the Soviets; Heeresgruppe Nord—200,000 men—is trapped in Courland.

September 19, 1944: Soviet Union signs Moscow Armistice with Finland.

December 24, 1944–February 13, 1945: Siege of Budapest; few German troops escape.

Weapons' development was a feature of the Eastern Front. The semi-automatic G43 rifle was based on captured Soviet weapons such as the SVT-40. In the background, a Panzerjäger II für 7.5cm Pak 40/2—Marder II. To the right, a Panther. *Bundesarchiv 101I-090-3912-07A*

January 12–February 2, 1945: The Vistula–Oder offensive sees Soviet forces advance through Poland into the Reich; Zhukov is 40 miles from Berlin.

January 13: Soviet offensive on East Prussia; Danzig falls on March 30, Königsberg on April 9.

February 2–24, 1945: Soviet Lower Silesian offensive. Breslau besieged.

March 15–31, 1945: Soviet Upper Silesian offensive.

March 16–April 15, 1945: Soviet offensive towards Vienna takes the city.

April 16–May 2, 1945: Soviet Berlin offensive starts with battles along the Oder and Neisse rivers, then Seelow Heights; by the 23rd Berlin is surrounded.

April 16–May 2, 1945: The Halbe pocket forms around 9. Armee that fights its way west; some 25,000 escape.

| Introduction

In the decades since the end of the war the German infantryman and his weaponry—a well-covered subject—has taken on almost mythical status. Even in defeat the German soldier is seen as a robust and cunning enemy beaten more by the numbers and firepower of the Allies than any failings of his own. This is a view reinforced and perpetuated by the influential postwar memoirs of various German commanders who were always more prepared to suggest that strategic defeat was in the face of their own tactical supremacy than accept their own errors or the accomplishments of their enemies.

Hitler's plans towards the east may not have been immediately apparent as Germany signed the Nazi-Soviet nonaggression pact, invaded and split Poland between them, and then attacked westwards. However, a quick look at *Mein Kampf* shows his views on the Soviet Union and its people: "common bloodstained criminals," " the scum of humanity," which "has exercised the most frightful regime of tyranny of all time. ... We must not forget that the international Jew, who today rules Russia absolutely, sees in Germany, not an ally, but a State marked for the same destiny." The Nazis thought that the only way for Germany to survive was to expand eastwards, populate the lands they captured, and either work the people they captured to death or expel them farther eastwards.

The economic exploitation of Soviet resources—agricultural produce and labor—was always part of the Nazi creed and the consequent deaths that would result were not considered reason to stop. Hitler expected his troops to be brutal, to extirpate resistance—military or civil—without compunction, and to mercilessly kill entire populations of whole districts in retaliation for partisan attacks. On the other hand, military authorities made it clear that crimes committed by German soldiers were not to be punished if they claimed to have ideological considerations as their motive. This was an open invitation for soldiers to behave brutally. And they did. Whether towards the obvious primary enemy, the Russian soldier, or towards the Soviet Union's many Jews, the German Army was directly involved in Nazi genocide assisting the four *SS-Einsatzgruppen* (task forces)—A, B, C, D—that followed them. The units were mainly SS, police, and auxiliaries from the local population. By the end of 1941, within the areas of the Soviet Union conquered by the Nazis, about half a million Jews had been murdered and between July and October 1941 as many as 600,000 POWs in Wehrmacht custody had been turned over to the SS to be killed. Those Soviet POWs who weren't shot were starved and worked or walked to death. The wounded were often shot on the spot.

Between 1941 and 1945 more than half the Soviet POWs (possibly as many as 3.3 million of 5.7 million) taken by the Germans died in captivity, many in concentration camps. German generals expected this. General Erich Hoepner:

> The objective of this battle must be the destruction of present-day Russia and it must therefore be conducted with unprecedented severity. Every military action

must be guided in planning and execution by an iron will to exterminate the enemy mercilessly and totally. In particular, no adherents of the present Russian-Bolshevik system are to be spared.

There were differences of opinion, however. General Joachim Lemelsen, commander of XLVII. Panzerkorps, wrote:

> This is murder! … The instruction of the Führer calls for ruthless action against Bolshevism (political commissars) and any kind of partisan! People who have been clearly identified as such should be taken aside and shot only by order of an officer … A Russian soldier who has been taken prisoner while wearing a uniform after he put up a brave fight, has a right to decent treatment.

The *Barbarossa* Decree of May 13, 1941

The Decree on the Jurisdiction of Martial Law and on Special Measures of the Troops was signed by Hitler's chief of staff on the OKW, Wilhelm Keitel. It covered the "Treatment of criminal acts committed by enemy civilians" and said that "Criminal acts committed by enemy civilians are withdrawn from the jurisdiction of courts martial and summary courts until further notice;" that "Partisans and guerrilla fighters must be mercilessly destroyed by the troops in battle or in pursuit;" and that "All other attacks by enemy civilians against the Wehrmacht, its members and service personnel must also be repelled by the troops on the spot by the most extreme measures up to the destruction of the attackers." As far as the treatment of criminal acts committed by members of the Wehrmacht and its service personnel against the local population, the decree said, "Prosecution for actions committed by members of the Wehrmacht and its service personnel against enemy civilians is not necessary even if these actions constitute a military crime or offense." It was, for the ordinary infantrymen, a license to kill indiscriminately.

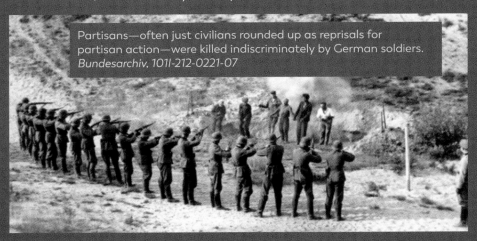

Partisans—often just civilians rounded up as reprisals for partisan action—were killed indiscriminately by German soldiers. *Bundesarchiv, 1011-212-0221-07*

On June 22, 1941, Hitler broke the Nazi-Soviet nonaggression pact signed in August 1939 and Germany invaded the Soviet Union. Everything seemed to proceed brilliantly as huge encirclement battles saw massive numbers of Soviet soldiers captured and their equipment destroyed or gained. The only niggle was timescale. Far from being over before winter, the German attacks bogged down in autumn mud thus giving the Soviets the time they needed to construct new defenses. This meant that when the frost hardened the ground sufficiently to allow the panzers to attack again, from November 14, the way to Moscow was barred.

While they had coped with the hot summer and disagreeable dust storms, the Germans didn't handle a Soviet winter very well and didn't know as much about the Soviet Union as they should have. For example, the Germans hadn't studied the reports of combat between Allies and the Soviets in the winter of 1918–19 when all the problems they would encounter had been identified. Indeed, before 1941 the German General Staff had never been interested in the history of wars in Northern and Eastern Europe.

> The older generation had been brought up in the tradition of von Moltke who considered it sufficient to study the countries immediately surrounding Germany … the northern regions of Europe remained practically unknown to the German soldier.

The resulting lack of awareness led to German soldiers suffering in the winter of 1941–42 and ultimately contributed to the failure of *Barbarossa*. In October and November 1941, the *rasputitsa*—muddy season following heavy rains—paralyzed the German logistical system, which was predicated on transporting supplies from railheads by trucks or horse-drawn vehicles. Five weeks elapsed before the going became firm enough for wheeled vehicles and the panzers.

Buoyed by the successes of 1939–41, Hitler and his generals had expected victory by the autumn, thus allowing many divisions to be sent elsewhere. The fact that the German Army was sitting in snow without winter clothing, which was in depots to the west, forced the Nazi Party to aim its Christmas drive at German civilians to collect winter clothes and skis for the front. Until they arrived in February 1942, German troops had to take clothes from corpses, and improvise—with devastating consequences. Everyone agrees about weather conditions in the east in October 1941, but there are conflicting accounts of the temperatures after that.

Maps and Mapping

Another factor that was to handicap the Germans was their lack of accurate information on the terrain. In Western Europe the Wehrmacht had fought over ground familiar to many of its commanders and well covered by accurate and detailed maps. Russia, however, was generally a great unknown. GFM (Generalfeldmarschall) Gerd von Rundstedt had this to say about the lack of accurate information: "I realized soon after the attack was begun that everything that had been written about Russia was nonsense. The maps we were given were all wrong. The roads that were marked nice and red and thick on a map turned out to be tracks, and what were tracks on the map became first-class roads. Even railways which were to be used by us simply didn't exist. Or a map would indicate that there was nothing in the area, and suddenly we would be confronted with an American-type town, with factory buildings and all the rest of it."

Extreme cold meant starting and maintaining vehicles was a nightmare—particularly tracked and halftracked vehicles. The German *Schachtellaufwerk* system of interweaved and overlapping wheels provided better load spread and so lower ground pressure and a better ride—but it wasn't easy to maintain, especially when jammed with frozen snow or mud. One of a series of watercolors of XXXXVII. Panzerkorps in the east by Fritz Brauner, an Obergefreiter in Flakregiment 101. *RCT*

Rasputitsa—the mud made the going impossible for motorized troops and stopped the German advance in its tracks. *NAC*

Fighting in the Russian Winter

The results of the decision to fight around Moscow without appropriate clothing and provisions highlighted the overoptimism of Hitler and the German planners. The lessons learned were identified in a series of U.S. Army pamphlets in the 1950s, most authored by high-ranking German sources:

- Mobility and logistical support were restricted because roads and runways could only be kept open by ploughing or compacting the snow. Cross-country transport—if possible, at all—required wide-tracked vehicles or sleds. Infantrymen moving through deep snow rapidly became exhausted. Extended marches required skis or at least snowshoes—but the wrong snowshoes were virtually useless.
- Without special lubricants firearms and motors froze up and became inoperative at subzero temperatures. Motor vehicles were unreliable; native horse sleighs provided the most reliable transport. By 1942–43, the Germans ensured they had suitable lubricants, but starting motor vehicles was a constant problem. Towing badly damaged both motors and differentials. Applying heat by lighting fires under engines for up to two hours before moving helped, as did just leaving motors running.
- Human efficiency and survival required adequate shelter. If not available locally, portable shelter had to be provided. Frostbite casualties exceeded battle losses unless troops wore proper clothing, including warm gloves and footgear. 6. Panzer-Division was reporting about 800 frostbite casualties a day in late 1941 until its engineers blasted craters for all the combat elements. Three to five men clustered in each foxhole which was covered with lumber and heated with an open fire. Frostbite cases all but disappeared. Speedy removal of the wounded from the battlefield to shelter was essential to prevent even minor wounds from resulting in death from exposure.
- The defensive was normally superior to the offensive because the attacker had to contend with debilitating exposure to frost and wind chill, exhaustion from moving through deep snow, relative lack of concealment, longer exposure to enemy fire because rushing was not feasible, and aggravated supply problems. Any offensive had to be limited in both time and distance— and had to have prospects of securing shelter.
- Troops not acclimated to the harsh environment had less chance for survival. Appropriate clothes and boots were essential, and their use required supervision: long overcoats were not practical for long marches; camouflage required white outer garments. Even though the temperature was very low, the sun's ultraviolet rays were greatly magnified and caused severe sunburn.
- The value of trained ski troops was underscored by their scarcity on both sides. The climate compounded distances. All deployments and maneuvers, especially cross-country, required extra time. Deep snow and ice complicated both retreat and pursuit. Where they had to cover open terrain in those operations, both sides found themselves in highly vulnerable positions.

Movement over ice had to be considered carefully in an area of extreme cold but if thick enough, it offered an excellent route.

· From 3 feet to 6 feet of snow nullified the killing power of small arms and when water was allowed to freeze over this, less thickness was needed. Deep snow reduced the effectiveness of mortar shells and low-caliber artillery and made the German 3.7cm and 5cm antitank artillery very difficult to use. During periods of extreme cold weapons formed a vapor when fired thus disclosing the shooting position. Almost anything warm—breath, smoke from a fire, a weapon firing—also caused vapor which tended to hang over a position thus disclosing it.

· Sound travels farther in very cold weather. The noise of troops advancing over heavy, crusted snow deprived them of the advantage of surprise. Canteens of water quickly froze if they were carried exposed. They had to be carried next to the body to keep from freezing and bursting. Charcoal was better than wood for heating because it created less smoke to reveal troop positions.

· Men had to be made to relieve themselves daily or constipation set in (although some were relieved at this as it stopped the flux caused by dysentery). Thaw periods created the greatest danger from trench foot. Great care had to be taken by every leader to ensure men were taking the proper precautions to guard against this: dry socks and constant exercise of the feet.

· Frozen ground made field fortifications difficult to construct. Explosives were useful for constructing foxholes and larger shelters, without which the infantry were at the mercy of the cold and enemy artillery. Mines often failed in winter. This was true when the snow was sufficiently deep to cushion the fuse and when alternating melting and freezing created an ice bridge over the detonator.

Skis spread the load to allow easier transport of weapons over ice and snow. This one is a "Doorknocker" 3.7cm antitank gun, so called because it did little more than announce its presence when used against the heavy armor of the T-34 or KV series Soviet tanks. *U.S. Army*

Russia isn't always frozen. Endless dusty marches in 1941 and the fertile cornfields of Ukraine in 1942 were features of the German summer advances. *NAC*

Generalfeldmarschall (GFM) Fedor von Bock, commander of Heeresgruppe Mitte, recorded in his war diary on November 5, 1941, a temperature of −29°C (−20°F). Marshal Zhukov, in Moscow, said that during the November offensive the temperature remained stable at −7° to −10°C (+19° to +14°F). Other Soviet figures cite meteorological service records of the minimum temperatures for the Moscow area in late 1941 as being October, −8.2°C (about +17°F); November, −17.3°C (+1°F); and December, −28.8°C (−20°F). There were also many reports of temperatures as low as −40° during that exceptionally cold winter, and at least one report of −53°C (−63°F).

One thing that is agreed is that the heavy snow started in December—just in time to help Heeresgruppe Mitte because the deep snow hindered the Soviet counteroffensive. The snow may have helped the Germans in the face of the Soviet counterattack, but the Ostheer suffered more than 734,000 casualties (about 23 percent of its average strength of 3,200,000 troops) during the first five months of the invasion, and on November 27, 1941, Generalmajor Eduard Wagner, the *Generalquartiermeister im OKH* (Quartermaster General of the German Army), reported that, "We are at the end of our resources in both personnel and materiel. We are about to be confronted with the dangers of deep winter."

By the turn of the year, they had suffered about 100,000 cases of frostbite, more than 14,000 of which required amputations. By the end of that terrible winter the number of frostbite victims exceeded a quarter of a million. To these must be added thousands of cases of pneumonia, influenza, and trench foot. The impact of those non-battle casualties made the disparity between the Germans and the Red Army more obvious. While the Soviets had lost millions in dead, wounded, and captured by December 1941, Russia was able to muster replacements from its vast manpower resources. In contrast, by November 26 German losses of about 375,000 dead, missing, and permanently disabled were virtually irreplaceable—they were the veterans, the canny NCOs, and junior officers who had fought so well in the early years. By April 1942 the German deficiency on the Soviet front had reached 625,000 men.

The German replacement troops had to change to take into account conditions on the Eastern Front. The first adjustment saw the army revise the standards for selecting lower-echelon commanders. Their average age was lowered, and the physical fitness requirements were raised. For weeks at a time officers and men had no baggage, no change of clothes and no opportunity to change their underwear. This required another type of adjustment to the Russian way of life, if only to prevail in the struggle against filth and vermin. Many officers and men of the older age groups broke down or became sick and had to be replaced by younger men. Certainly, the Soviets were seemingly able to put up with more than their German counterparts.

Introduction

Carrot and Stick

Morale is an important consideration in any army, and many methods are used to foster it. Among the "carrots" are decorations, which supply a tangible record of soldiers' bravery and honor and are awarded by most armies. The photos of German soldiers on the Eastern Front show how important medals are. Few—even in the dirtiest, hardest environments—do not have their decorations visible, the most often seen being those that defined the infantryman: the Close Combat Clasp, General Assault Badge, Tank Destruction Badge, and Wound Badge. Below are the most often seen:

- Antiaircraft Flak Battle Badges for both Luftwaffe and Army (*Flakkampfabzeichen der Luftwaffe/des Heeres*), and the Ground Assault Badge of the Luftwaffe (*Erdkampfabzeichen der Luftwaffe*). The two Flak badges were awarded for action against aircraft, although the Luftwaffe's was also for ground targets. The Ground Assault Badge of the Luftwaffe was instituted on March 31, 1942.
- Bandit-warfare Badge (*Bandenkampfabzeichen*) was awarded from January 29, 1944. There were three classes: bronze (20 combat days: 1,650 awarded), silver (50: 510) and gold (100: 47), ten of the latter being awarded in February and March 1945 to members of the 24. Waffen-Gebirgs-(Karstjäger-) Division der SS.
- Close Combat Clasp (*Nahkampfspange*): three grades: bronze for 15 battles, silver for 25, gold for 50+. The gold was highly regarded by soldiers and was bestowed personally by Hitler. Numbers issued: 36,400 bronze, 9,500 silver, and 631 gold. It was awarded in "recognition to the soldier who often engages in close man to man combat with weapon in hand and has proven his worth."
- Eastern Front Medal (*Medaille, Winterschlacht im Osten* 1941/42). Over 3 million were awarded "in recognition of proficiency in combat against the Bolshevik enemy and the Russian winter during the period November 15, 1941 to April 15, 1942."

Franz Giesler was a highly decorated soldier who was awarded the *Eisernes Kreuz* (Iron Cross) *I. Klasse* on March 16, 1942, *Deutsches Kreuz in Gold* on May 28, 1944, as a Leutnant in 5./Grenadier-Regiment 457, and the *Ritterkreuz* on April 29, 1945, as a Hauptmann in I./Flak-Regiment 120 (although the latter medal wasn't recognized). In this photo he wears the *Ritterkreuz* at his neck, the *Eisernes Kreuz II. Klasse* at the second buttonhole of his tunic and *Deutsches Kreuz in Gold* on his right breast pocket. Above his left breast pocket is the *Nahkampfspange*, below which he wears the *Eisernes Kreuz I. Klasse*, *Infanterie-Sturmabzeichen* and *Verwundetenabzeichen*. On his right arm he has two *Sonderabzeichen für das Niederkämpfen von Panzerkampfwagen durch Einzelkämpfer. RCT*

15

Above left: The Infantry Assault Badge in silver could be awarded to infantrymen and Gebirgsjäger. The bronze class was instituted for motorized infantry and the machine-gun, infantry gun, and antitank companies of infantry or Gebirgsjäger regiments. *RCT*

Above center and right: Eastern Front Medal and award notification, this one to Leutnant Herbert Vögel of 2. Panzer-Aufklärungs-Abteilung. *RCT*

- General Assault Badge (*Allgemeines Sturmabzeichen*): one grade; later (1943) adapted by adding a plate identifying 25, 50, 75, or 100 attacks. Over 460,000 awarded by divisional commanders to officers, non-commissioned officers and enlisted personnel who had been involved in three assaults or three different days of fighting "gun in hand". Successful violent exploration as well as counterattacks also counted. Members of the artillery, tank destroyer teams and members of StuG batteries could also be awarded the medal.
- German Army Parachutist Badge (*Fallschirmschützen-Abzeichen des Heeres*).
- German Cross (*Deutsches Kreuz*): two grades, gold and silver.
- Honor Roll Clasp of the Army (*Ehrenblatt des Heeres*). First issued in July 1941, the roll recorded the names of soldiers who had distinguished themselves in combat in an exceptional way. Until January 30, 1944, it was a paper award only. Four additional grades introduced on November 10, 1944, based on the number of combat operations—2nd for 25 eligible operations, 3rd for 50, 4th for 75, and 5th for 100. It was awarded to those who had already received the Iron Cross in both the first and second class and had distinguished themselves in combat. 4,556 awarded to German Army and Waffen-SS soldiers.
- Infantry Assault Badge (*Infanterie-Sturmabzeichen*): silver for footsoldiers (infantry and *Gebirgsjäger*—mountain troops); bronze created in June 1940 for motorized and mechanized troops. Awarded to army and Waffen-SS from January 1, 1940; authorized at regimental level, it was for those who had participated in infantry assaults on at least three separate days of battle on the front line. 941,000 issued.
- Iron Cross (*Eisernes Kreuz*): three grades: the Iron Cross (two versions, II. *Klasse*—4.5 million awarded—saw only the ribbon worn from the second tunic buttonhole; I. *Klasse*—300,000 awarded—was a pin-on medal), the Knight's Cross (*Ritterkreuz*

various versions; 7,313 in total awarded), and the Grand Cross (*Großkreuz*, only awarded to Göring). The iconic German award, the Iron Cross was a German version of an earlier Prussian award. The Clasp to the Iron Cross (*Spange zum Eisernen Kreuz*) was awarded to those who had been awarded the Iron Cross in World War I and was awarded again in World War II. Over 100,000 were awarded.

- Luftwaffe Panzer Battle Badge (*Panzerkampfabzeichen der Luftwaffe*): silver for tank crew, black for panzergrenadiers and crews of other armored vehicles.
- Panzer Battle Badge (*Panzerkampfabzeichen*): silver for tank crew, bronze (instituted June 6, 1940) for panzergrenadiers and crews of other armored vehicles.
- Parachute Rifleman's Badge (*Fallschirmschützenabzeichen*).
- Sharpshooter's Badge (*Scharfschützenabzeichen*): third class (no cord) for 20 witnessed kills, second class (silver cord) for 40, first class (gold cord) for 60.
- Tank Destruction Badge (*Sonderabzeichen für das Niederkämpfen von Panzer-kampfwagen durch Einzelkämpfer*): gold for five tanks (replacing four silver badges when the fifth was destroyed). It was awarded from June 22, 1941, to a soldier who, as a lone fighter, knocked out an enemy tank with close-combat weapons. From December 18, 1943, this was extended to include Panzerschreck and Panzerfaust. 421 gold issued.
- War Merit Cross (*Kriegsverdienstkreuz*): four degrees; related civil decoration.

Campaign Shields

During World War II, Germany awarded campaign shields for particularly hard-fought campaigns—for example, the *Narvikschild* for the battle of Narvik fought April 9–June 8, 1940. The following five shields were instituted, produced, awarded, and worn in recognition of significant battles on the Eastern Front. Others, for the battles of Memel and Warsaw, may have been awarded but were not produced before the end of the war.

- *Cholmschild*: Resupplied by air, Kampfgruppe Scherer held out at Cholm from January 21 to May 5, 1942, until the siege was lifted. 5,500 were awarded.

Verwundetenabzeichen (Wound Badge)

This was awarded "As an honor to those who were wounded by the enemy while bravely committing themselves for the Fatherland." It came in three forms: black (3rd class), for those wounded once or twice; silver (2nd class) wounded three or four times; and gold (1st class, which could be awarded posthumously) five times or more. The regulations went into some detail as to the type of wounds applicable to each level, the gold involving the loss of both hands or legs, the loss of a hand or foot in three or more limbs, the loss of a leg and a hand, the loss or total blindness of both eyes (finger counting is no longer possible), and cerebral/spinal cord injuries with severe functional disorders. 2.5 million received the black, a million the silver, and 500,000 the gold. *RCT*

A Gebirgsjäger NCO in the Caucasus, 1942. He's carrying both classes of the *Eisernes Kreuz*, an *Infanterie-Sturmabzeichen* and *Verwundetenabzeichen 3. Klasse* (in black). Note the *Edelweiß* badge on his *Feldmütze*. NAC

Below: *Cholmschild. RCT*

Left: General Joachim Lemelsen decorates Generalmajor Walter von Boltenstern with the Ritterkreuz on March 13, 1941. NARA

Below: *Demjanskschild. RCT*

- *Demjankschild*: Over 100,000 men were trapped in the Demyansk pocket between February 8 and April 21, 1942; sustained by air, it convinced Göring and Hitler that the Luftwaffe could resupply this sort of pocket. In fact, the air losses would go on to haunt the Luftwaffe when it tried to resupply 6. Armee in Stalingrad. 100,000 were awarded.
- *Krimschild*: The Crimean campaign lasted from September 26, 1941, to July 4, 1942, when Sevastopol fell. 250,000 Crimean shields were awarded.
- *Kubanschild*: From February to October 1943, German 17. Armee attempted to maintain a bridgehead against Soviet 4th Ukrainian Front. Many were awarded.
- *Lapplandschild*: Produced postwar for members of 20. Gebirgsarmee.

Penalties

As one would expect of the Nazi regime, alongside the "carrots" they were prepared to use a big "stick." Among the many examples of the more draconian penalties, the *Strafbataillone*—penal battalions—were administered by the Feldgendarmerie and later by the Feldjägerkorps. Forced to undertake suicidal missions—mine clearance for example—or those where high casualties were expected, men who succeeded and survived were allowed to rejoin ordinary units. By the end of the war, 50,000 had served in these battalions.

Rehabilitation units saw soldiers who had been sentenced to serve extended prison terms but who showed promise of reforming put on parole and transferred to improvised rehabilitation platoons, companies, or battalions. These were committed at critical points of the front. The rehabilitation units had particularly efficient NCOs and officers and often gave a good account of themselves. In 1944 one of these rehabilitation battalions fought exceptionally well in the encircled fortress of Ternopol in eastern Galicia. When the town fell, several noncommissioned officers and men of this battalion fought their way back to their own lines under great hazards and hardships.

The German Army executed many of its own solders for desertion (22,500 were sentenced to death with 15,000 usually the quoted figure of executions, although it was likely higher) and many others were executed for insubordination, defeatism, or bad-mouthing Adolf Hitler or the war (figures quoted from 23,000–50,000). Most of the condemned who weren't executed died in prison.

Sippenhaft—kin liability—stems from an old idea which threatens that the family of anyone who commits an offense may also be punished. The worst examples are the excesses after the July 20 bomb plot, but perhaps a more typical example is of panzergrenadier Wenzel Leiss who was captured at Stalingrad (he returned to Germany in 1949). Trumped-up charges—and no judicial sentence—saw his pregnant wife, 2-year-old daughter, and five members of his family sent to Sachsenhausen concentration camp where they were executed. Another well-known occasion of *Sippenhaft* was the arrest of the family of General Otto Lasch, commander of Festung Königsberg, after the city surrendered.

Sketch by Ernst Eigener of a German Gefreiter (one chevron, one pip = Gefreiter with more than six years' service). Note grenade in boot and entrenching tool in belt—neither typical but adding to the overall composition. *RCT*

Partisan Warfare

The Germans got it wrong from the start. The planning for *Barbarossa* was based on a short campaign and there was very little consideration of what might happen in the rear areas. The three *Befehlshaber des rückwärtigen Heeresgebietes* (Army Group Rear Area Commands) were supposed to pass quickly on to the civilian administration. Run by the *Kommandant rückwärtiges Armeegebiet* (Korück), they would be policed by the Wehrmacht *Sicherungs* (Security) *Divisionen*—made up of "mainly older, relatively poorly-equipped soldiers of dubious quality, wholly insufficient quantity and low priority in terms of training, equipment and supply." These divisions worked hand in glove with the SS-Einsatzgruppen, (already mentioned), the Wehrmacht's *Geheime Feldpolizei* (secret police) and the *Ordnungspolizei* (Order Police, see p. 34). This plan didn't take into consideration the fact that there were areas of the Soviet Union—Ukraine in particular—where the advancing Germans were greeted as liberators or that there were strong pockets of anti-Communist feeling.

The OKW and German Army had very similar views on partisans: shoot first and ask questions later. As far as OKW was concerned,

Insidious partisan warfare can be destroyed only with the greatest resoluteness and a lack of consideration for all mitigating factors. Good-naturedness is stupidity and softness can be criminal. The partisans will be shot and the execution will be ordered by an officer. A dead partisan accomplishes nothing.

Heeresgruppe Mitte felt:

In the event of partisan activity, two Russian civilians should be shot for every German soldier killed and three civilians would be executed for every important German facility attacked. Furthermore, any Russian civilians found near railway or road bridges after the nighttime curfew should be shot on sight.

This attitude—and Soviet successes—saw the partisan movement grow. They avoided open combat as much as possible, concentrating on sabotaging German lines of communication—mining highways, demolishing railway tracks, attacking trains, looting railway cars, raiding trucks and convoys, burning rations, ammunition, and fuel depots, and cutting telephone lines—and then attacking the soldiers who came to fix the problem.

Disrupting railway lines was of particular importance. An excerpt from the monthly report of the transport chief of Heeresgruppe Mitte, covering the period August 1–31, 1943, said:

Despite the employment of special alert units for the protection of the railroad lines, partisan activity increased by 25 percent during August 1943 and reached a record of 1,392 incidents as compared with 1,114 for July. ... Individual demolition points amounted to 20,505, while 4,528 mines were removed. During the night from August 2 to 3 the partisans began to put into effect a program of large-scale destruction. Numerous demolitions were carried out which caused a serious curtailment of all railroad traffic and a considerable loss of railroad materiel. Within two nights the 6–7,000 miles of track in the area were cut in 8,422 places, while another 2,478 mines were detected and removed prior to exploding. Several lines could not be put back into operation for a considerable time.

Another important example took place during the night of June 19–20, 1944—just before the start of Soviet Operation *Bagration*. In the area of Heeresgruppe Mitte the partisans attempted 15,000 demolitions on railroad lines and were successful in 10,500 cases. Their main effort was directed against 3. Panzerarmee supply lines, the same unit that would bear the brunt of the Red Army attack. The result was that all double-track lines were blocked for a period of 24 hours; single-track lines were interrupted for over 48 hours. It was a good example of the coordination between the Red Army and partisan headquarters.

These were the exceptions, however. Most of the partisan attacks were less damaging—pinpricks rather than major blows. Ben Shepherd's analysis of the effects on the 221. Sicherungs-Division identifies the growth of the numbers of partisans in Belorussia (from 130,000 to 250,000) and the number of acts of sabotage (87 in April; 233 in May). Between June 21, 1942, and May 31, 1943, 296 Germans and 197 "native allies" were killed and a similar number wounded by the partisans. In the same period, retribution saw 1,523 "partisans" killed. Locally, that led to burning of villages and shooting of "accomplices." But also—as in Yugoslavia—it elicited more significant responses. There were several major sweeps—*Großunternehmen*, "large-scale encircle-and-destroy operations which became the main source of carnage in the anti-partisan campaign from 1942"—during which the indiscriminate killing of civilians and partisans did more to foster anti-German and pro-partisan sentiment than any attempts by the Soviet commissars. Examples of such sweeps in the Heeresgruppe Mitte area were *Unternehmen Zigeunerbaron* (Gipsy Baron) May 15–June 6, 1943, and *Unternehmen Freischütz* (Marksman) May 21–30, both by elements of 2. Panzerarmee around Bryansk. Other operations took place before the launch of *Unternehmen Zitadelle* (Citadel). In January–June 1944 *Unternehmen Regenschauer* (Rain Shower), *Frühlingsfest* (Spring Festival), and *Kormoran* (Cormorant) saw 3. Panzerarmee clear partisans in the Ushachi area of Byelorussia.

The gold version of the Bandit-warfare Badge was reserved for award by Reichsführer-SS Heinrich Himmler in person. *Armémuseum Stockholm Sweden/ WikiCommons (CC-BY-4.0)*

| The Soldier

The German soldiers who crossed into the Soviet Union in June 1941 could never have anticipated what they were letting themselves in for. They expected to be victorious. In two and a half remarkable years they had defeated every foe they had come up against, and this gave them huge belief in their weapons, their leaders and their training. They had been indoctrinated to believe in Nazism and their Führer and would do everything asked of them to defeat the enemy and eradicate the world of Jews, Bolsheviks and any *Untermenschen* (subhumans) who stood in the way of their Aryan destiny.

The Germans of 1939 lived in a militarized society whose young men under the Nazis had been schooled with war in mind. Toughened up by stints in the *Hitlerjugend* (Hitler Youth)—which had eight million members in 1939—and the *Reichsarbeitsdienst* (RAD—Reich Labor Service), they were then carefully trained for war during their period of conscripted service. Hitler reintroduced this in 1935 when the period of active service was fixed at one year. This was extended to two years in August 1936 for all men aged 18–45.

When German youths were inducted for military service, most of them had already had the equivalent of basic military training, were in excellent physical condition, and had been indoctrinated both with Nazi ideology and military attitudes. As a result, their training period as conscripts could move very rapidly through the preliminary stages; in two or three months the conscripts could take part in maneuvers involving divisions or armies. Because of the work done by the Hitlerjugend and the RAD, the two-year (prewar) training in the army could advance much more rapidly and effectively. Furthermore, German boys had received good opportunities to practice and develop qualities of leadership, and officer material was already clearly marked out by the time they reached military age.

The training took place in the *Ersatzheer* (Replacement Army) before recruits moved on to the *Feldheer* (Field Army). The emphasis was on physical fitness; weapons training with marksmanship was an important component. The training lasted 16 weeks and included fire and movement, command, ballistics, heavy weapons, and tactical field training, map reading, fieldcraft, and camouflage.

Whilst there were many civilian shooting clubs in Germany, all recruits had to start from scratch. A raised firing platform was used when learning how to fire from prone. The weapon would be an Erma Erfurt single-shot .22 version of the K98 or a K98 fitted with an EL24 .22 barrel insert. From the rifle the recruit would progress to machine guns. *RCT*

Über allem steht die Deutsche Infanterie—with overtones of the national anthem, this recruiting poster extols: "Above all stands the German Infantry." The images show: The March (*Marsch*)—The march of the infantry sets the tempo of the battle; The Defense (*Abwehr*)—The enemy attack shatters against the tough defense of the infantry; The Attack (*Angriff*)—At the critical point of the battle, the infantry charges irresistibly; The Victory (*Sieg*)—The crowning glory of the hard infantry battle is victory. Recruiting for the infantry became progressively more difficult as the war went on and casualties rose. *Via Hennepin Country Library, Minnesota, Digital Collections*

Truppenführung (Leading Troops)

This manual was published in two parts (in 1933 and 1934) and is often cited as a major contributor to German military success. It shows remarkable foresight, having sections on tanks and aircraft at a time when other countries hadn't taken on board the lessons of World War I—in particular, the shock tactics used in the *Michael* offensive of March 1918. It isn't an instruction manual per se, but a manual aimed at the NCO and junior officer that stresses the need for versatility; that the infantry officer must familiarize himself with the capacities of other arms than his own—a combined-arms view of fighting that certainly assisted the elements of *Kampfgruppen* (ad hoc formations of troops often collected from different services, or battle groups) to work together. It stresses that subordinates should use their initiative and provides a mission-oriented approach to leadership tactics—*Auftragstaktik*. There is little about strategy—something at which the German high command did not excel—or what to do when your command structure is compromised by heavy losses. It is important also to note that Hitler's continuous meddling with low-level command decisions did much to negate the precepts of *Truppenführung*. These excerpts give a flavor of the work:

- The conduct of war is based on continuous development. New means of warfare call forth ever changing employment. Their use must be anticipated, their influence must be correctly estimated and quickly utilized. Situations in war are of unlimited variety. Friction and mistakes are of everyday occurrence.
- The teaching of the conduct of war cannot be concentrated exhaustively in regulations. The principles so enunciated must be employed dependent upon the situation. Simplicity of conduct, logically carried through, will most surely attain the objective.
- The example and personal conduct of officers and noncommissioned officers are of decisive influence on the troops. The officer who in the face of the enemy is cold-blooded, decisive, and courageous inspires his troops onward. Mutual trust is the surest basis of discipline in necessity and danger. The leaders must live with their troops, participate in their dangers, their wants, their joys, their sorrows. Only in this way can they estimate the battle worth and the requirements of the troops.
- Superior battle worth can equalize numerical inferiority. The higher the battle worth, the more vigorous and versatile can war be executed. Superior leadership and superior troop battle readiness are reliable portents of victory. Troops only superficially welded together, and not through long training and experience, more easily fail under severe conditions and under unexpected crises.
- The first demand in war is decisive action. Everyone, the highest commander and the most junior soldier, must be aware that omissions and neglects incriminate him more severely than the mistake of choice of means. Great successes presume boldness and daring preceded by good judgment.

Training didn't stop when you joined your unit. Here, an NCO demonstrates how to use the Pzf 30 (gross) Panzerfaust. The small version had entered service in 1943; the large (*gross*) in mid-1944. Its effective range was 30 meters. *Bundesarchiv 1011-700-0258-22A*

- We never have at our disposal all the desired forces for the decisive action. The weaker force, through speed, mobility, great march accomplishments, utilization of darkness and the terrain to the fullest, surprise and deception, can be the stronger at the decisive area.
- Time and space must be correctly estimated, favorable situations quickly recognized and decisively exploited. Every advantage over the enemy increases our own freedom of action. Rapidity of action in the displacement of troops can be assisted greatly or retarded by the roads and street nets and by the terrain conditions. The season, the weather, the condition of the troops, are also of influence.
- The duration of strategical and tactical operations cannot always be foreseen. Successful engagements often proceed slowly. Often the success of today's battle is first recognized tomorrow. Surprising the enemy is a decisive factor in a success.
- The mission and the situation form the basis of the action. The mission designates the objective. The leader must never forget his mission. A mission which indicates several tasks easily diverts from the main objective. Obscurity of the situation is the rule. Seldom can one have exact information of the enemy. Clarification of the hostile situation is a self-evident demand. However, to wait in tense situations for information is seldom a token of strong leadership, more often of weakness.
- The decision arises from the mission and the situation. Should the mission no longer suffice as the fundamental of conduct or if it is changed by events, the decision must take these considerations into account. Timely recognition of the conditions and the time which call for a new decision is an attribute of the art of leadership. The commander must permit freedom of action to his subordinates insofar as this does not endanger the whole scheme. He must not surrender to them those decisions for which he alone is responsible.

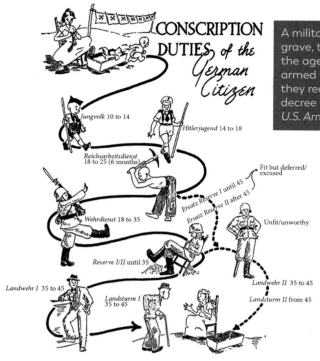

CONSCRIPTION DUTIES of the German Citizen

Jungvolk 10 to 14

Hitlerjugend 14 to 18

Reichsarbeitsdienst 18 to 25 (6 months)

Fit but deferred/excused

Ersatz Reserve I until 45

Ersatz Reserve II after 45

Wehrdienst 18 to 35

Unfit/unworthy

Reserve I/II until 35

Landwehr I 35 to 45

Landwehr II 35 to 45

Landsturm I 35 to 45

Landsturm II from 45

A militarized society from the cradle to the grave, the Nazi credo was that males from the age of 10 were prepared for service in the armed forces. They stayed on the books until they reached 55 although the Volkssturm decree would see that extended to 60.
U.S. Army

Undoubtedly, the German Army of 1939 was well trained, well equipped and well motivated, its young men having been schooled under the Nazis; many of its officers were experienced soldiers. In the interwar period the Germans had embraced new technology and learned lessons from World War I in a way that the Allies—particularly the British—had not. The exigencies of war, however, meant that this level of training couldn't be kept up and later in the war the standards weren't as high. The German Army itself had a very strong ésprit de corps that continued to the bitter end. On March 15, 1945, the U.S. War Department produced a handbook on the Wehrmacht. Its opening section on the German soldier discusses their continued defiance in the face of defeat:

After five and a half years of ever-growing battle against ever-stronger enemies, the German Army in 1945 looks, at first glance, much the worse for wear. It is beset on all sides and is short of everything. It has suffered appalling casualties and must resort to old men, boys, invalids, and unreliable foreigners for its cannon fodder. Its weapons and tactics seem not to have kept pace with those of the armies opposing it; its supply system in the field frequently breaks down. Its position is obviously hopeless, and it can only be a question of time until the last German soldier is disarmed, and the once proud German Army of the great Frederick and of Scharnhorst, of Ludendorff and of Hitler, exists no more as a factor to be reckoned with.

Yet this shabby, war-weary machine has struggled on in a desperate effort to postpone its inevitable demise. … Despite the supposed chronic disunity at the top, disaffection among the officer corps, and disloyalty in the rank and file, despite the acute lack of weapons, ammunition, fuel, transport, and human reserves, the German Army seems to function with its old precision and to overcome what appear to be insuperable difficulties with remarkable speed. Only by patient and incessant hammering from all sides can its collapse be brought about.

The cause of this toughness, even in defeat, is not generally appreciated. It goes much deeper than the quality of weapons, the excellence of training and leadership, the soundness of tactical and strategic doctrine, or the efficiency of control at all echelons. It is to be found in the military tradition which is so deeply ingrained

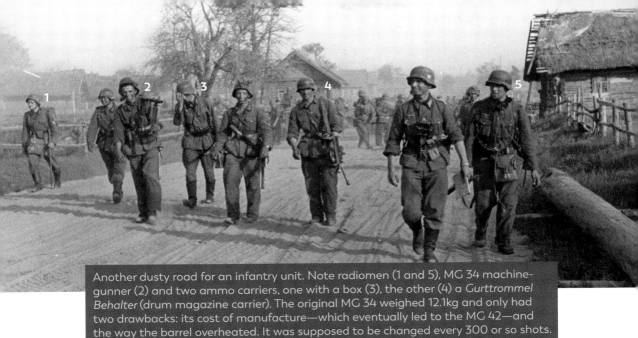

Another dusty road for an infantry unit. Note radiomen (1 and 5), MG 34 machine-gunner (2) and two ammo carriers, one with a box (3), the other (4) a *Gurttrommel Behalter* (drum magazine carrier). The original MG 34 weighed 12.1kg and only had two drawbacks: its cost of manufacture—which eventually led to the MG 42—and the way the barrel overheated. It was supposed to be changed every 300 or so shots. This could be quickly accomplished but was still a problem in combat. *NAC*

in the whole character of the German nation and which alone makes possible the interplay of these various factors of strength to their full effectiveness.

The Germans, themselves, remember the morale of the last years of the war despite the propaganda aimed at them by the Soviets. General von Senger und Etterlin said:

> I can only say the morale, in spite of these terrible losses and terrible times which we had to endure, was high. Which means we always felt superior to the Soviets. We always thought we were much better than they were. Our command and control was much better. Also, the single private soldier felt immensely superior to them as long as unit coherence existed and as long as the man was not completely isolated, lonely or something. It happened occasionally that these people lost their confidence, but very few were like that. Actually, there was absolutely no problem at all.

The sizable German forces used in the east were made up primarily of German Army and Waffen-SS divisions; in total some 330 infantry divisions were raised during the war and the vast majority served in the east. For the start of *Unternehmen Barbarossa*, the Wehrmacht deployed 120 infantry divisions (out of 175 in total in June 1941), 14 motorized infantry divisions and 19 tank divisions—a total of 3,680 tanks and 2.5 million men.

Manpower

	Axis total	*German (% in east)*	*Red Army Forces*
Jun 1941	3,767,000	3,117,000 (71%)	2,680,000 (in theater)
			5,500,000 (overall)
Jun 1942	3,720,000	2,690,000 (80%)	5,313,000
Jul 1943	3,933,000	3,483,000 (63%)	6,724,000
Jun 1944	3,370,000	2,520,000 (62%)	6,425,000
Jan 1945	2,330,000	2,230,000 (60%)	6,532,000
Apr 1945	1,960,000		6,410,000
Total mobilized			34,476,700

German army divisions were mobilized in deployment waves (*Aufstellungswellen*), with each wave structured slightly differently depending on availability and the tables of organization in force at the time of their mobilization. The first four waves were available in 1939 and provided 85 divisions.

Wave	Divisions	Active	% personnel Reservists	Landwehr
1	35	78%	18% (12% Class I, 6% Class II)	4%
2	16	6%	91% (83% Class I, 8% Class II)	3%
3	20	1%	58% (12% Class I, 46% Class II)	42%
4	14	8%	68% (21% Class I, 47% Class II)	24%

The personnel differences meant different levels of training, with the divisions of the 1st and 2nd waves ready for active service and those of the 3rd and 4th waves requiring more training. The divisions of the 1st wave were fully equipped as per their tables of organization. Subsequently, succeeding waves—there were 25 in all—had reduced manpower, lacked certain weapons, particularly artillery, or had to make do with older or captured vintage weapons.

The infantry came in various forms: the standard *Infanterie-Division*, whose infantrymen—the *Landser* (the term usually referred to an enlisted soldier of some experience: i.e., not recruits and not officers)—served in *Infanterie-Regimente*. After 1942 these regiments became grenadier regiments. Infantrymen in panzer divisions started out in *Schützen* regiments. When the general infantry became *Grenadiere*, the *Schützen* regiments (and the men within them) became *Panzergrenadiere*.

The other main types of infantry were *Fallschirmjäger* (airborne), *Gebirgsjäger* (mountain infantry), *Jäger* (light infantry—*Skijäger* could use skis), *Bodenständig* (static—used, for example, as garrisons or for coastal defense), and *Sicherheits* (security divisions) which were configured for

The Skijäger arm badge was worn on the right upper arm of those infantrymen who had qualified in the use of skis. *RCT*

Packhorses carrying small-arms ammunition on their *Tragtiersattel* carrying frames pass Skijäger, possibly from the 1. Skijäger-Division which was raised exclusively for the Eastern Front in autumn 1943. *NAC*

KÖZÖS ERŐVEL A BOLSEVIZMUS ELLEN
EURÓPA ÉS MAGYARORSZÁG FENNMARADÁSÁÉRT!

FALLSCHIRMJÄGER
MELDUNG BEIM DISZIPLINARVORGESETZTEN

Above left: Propaganda in Budapest, 1944: "Together against Bolshevism. For the Survival of Europe and Hungary." The fourth member of the Axis powers, Hungary's politics had become more right wing in the 1930s. The reward for joining was territorial gains including chunks of Czechoslovakia, Romania, Slovakia and, after the joint German-Hungarian invasion in April 1941, Yugoslavia. *Fortepan–Lissák Tivadar*

Above right: The German airborne troops saw little use as paratroops on the Eastern Front. Their undoubted fighting ability made them superb infantry and they saw extensive use as ground troops in the east. *SF collection*

security and anti-partisan operations in the rear areas of the armies, especially in the USSR. From the 32nd wave, raised in 1944–45, the *Volksgrenadier* (VD) divisions were formed from replacement troops, sometimes around a cadre of veterans, with reduced manpower (their regiments had two rather than three battalions) and often with older personnel. While many of these units were ineffective, some proved to be excellent such as the 549th VD Division under Oberst Karl Jank that fought in Lithuania, Prussia, and Germany before surrendering to American troops in Mecklenberg

Typical of the Nazi regime, there were overlapping responsibilities and command structures, the most obvious being the Waffen-SS, whose tactical control came under the OKW although Himmler, the Reichsführer-SS, exerted control too. There were 38 Waffen-SS divisions, many of the later units recruited in the east—there were Ukrainian, Latvian, Estonian, Russian, and Hungarian divisions—and a number from the Balkans as well as those from other West European countries.

From 1942 the Luftwaffe contributed to the need for extra infantry by creating the *Luftwaffefelddivisionen* (air force divisions). They came under army tactical control but initially under Luftwaffe administrative control. However, they performed nowhere near as well as the Fallschirmjäger, who proved to be among the toughest German soldiers, and the Flak battalions, particularly those equipped with the 8.8cm, which became the mainstay against the T-34s—indeed, by 1943 two Luftwaffe *Flak-Korps* were supporting the Ostheer.

Most *Luftwaffefelddivisionen* served on the Eastern Front in winter 1942–43. They weren't the most effective troops—the lower army ranks labeled them "*Luftwaffen-Fehlkonstruktions-Divisionen*" or "mistakenly constructed air force divisions." Many of these divisions suffered heavy losses and were disbanded in 1943 and 1944 and transferred to the army. Some of the survivors volunteered to join the Fallschirmjäger but the majority formed army divisions reorganized along the lines of the Type 1944 infantry division (see below) with their Luftwaffe officers replaced by army men. The new divisions had three Jäger regiments each with two battalions, a 13. Kompanie (assault guns) and 14. Kompanie (antitank guns). The army added a reconnaissance battalion that later became a fusilier battalion.

Before discussing the components of the German infantry divisions, it's important to be aware of the difference between a table of organization and the reality on the ground. While a division may have a nominal strength of, say, 17,500, it is very unlikely that is its true strength. The most obvious cause for this is death or wounding; other reasons include lack of replacements, illness, leave, training, or promotion to another unit. The German Army had a multiplicity of terms used when reporting strength: *Sollstärke* (authorized strength according to tables of organization), *Iststärke* (actual strength including those temporarily absent), *Fehlstellen* (unfilled positions), *Gefechtsstärke* (fighting strength including drivers and co-drivers of combat vehicles—any fit personnel), and *Verpflegungsstärke* (ration strength including numbers of horses and non-fighting elements such as medical, staff, and supply train personnel). Finally, there was *Tagesstärke*—the strength on the day of the report including temporary attachments—and *Kampfstärke*, the teeth of the unit, the combat strength, the fighting men but not artillery or admin. That final figure was usually substantially less than commanders would have liked. In Russia, battalions with a *Kampfstärke* of over 400 men were considered strong. The other factor was *Kampfwert*—battle value—which had four levels starting at suitable for offense and went down to conditionally suitable for defense.

As the war dragged on the shortage of manpower became a crucial factor for the German Army. Between 1941 and 1943 the infantry division was reduced in strength from c. 17,500 to 15,000. The Type 1944 Infantry Division (*Infanterie-Division Kriegestat* 44)

The Reality of Unit Strengths

An example showing Grenadier-Regiment 7 and its weapons in early 1945.

Strength

	Offr	NCOs	ORs	TOTAL	Auxiliaries	Horses
11.01.45 Ration	24	280	1015	1319	136	569
11.01.45 Combat	21	185	802	1008	–	141
21.01.45 Combat	17	95	492	604	–	137
01.02.45 Combat	16	98	395	509	–	131

Weapons

	LMG	SMG	Mortars 8 + 12cm	Infantry guns 7.5 + 15cm	PAKs 7.5cm	Bazookas
11.01.45	45	12	9 + 5	6 + 2	3	15
21.01.45	12	3	6 + 5	4 + 2	2	12
01.02.45	23	1	2 + 5	4 + 1	2	12
11.02.45	16	–	2 + 5	7 + 1	2	10
21.02.45	10	–	4 + –	6 + 1	1	10

saw the infantry regiments each lose a battalion (two in each rather than three) and rifle companies lose a squad (three in each rather than four). The reconnaissance battalion was replaced by a fusilier battalion with heavy weapons and an infantry company mounted on bicycles to provide the division's reconnaissance. The Type 1944 division's *Sollstärke* was 12,772.

From early in the campaign the Germans improvised ways of increasing infantry numbers by trawling through supply and service units for suitable men. One problem caused by this was the lack of suitable infantry training which, perforce, reduced combat efficiency.

However, this was alleviated by assigning each division a field replacement training battalion—although when push came to shove these battalions were also thrust into the front line as were army training schools. Other expedients included looking at artillery, antitank, armored, signaling and engineer units; but taking men from these technical arms led to its own problems as it reduced skill levels.

In mid-1944, after Operation *Bagration* and the battle of Normandy had decimated the army, some 50 new Volksgrenadier divisions were raised: the Sollstärke of these was 10,072. There was another iteration, the Type 1945 Infantry Division (*Infanterie-Division Kriegestat 45*), but they didn't see combat before the war ended.

Infantry Engineers

During assault operations, especially when they involved fortified positions or bunkers, there were tasks that the regular infantrymen struggled to perform—particularly when they involved demolitions. To cater for these problems, the assault detachments were accompanied by engineers. Other important tasks for infantry engineers were:

- Mine detection and removal. The main electronic mine detectors were Frankfurt 42 and Wien 41.
- Mine laying (antitank/personnel).
- Obstacle construction.
- Crossing waterways by boat or improvised means.
- Building light bridges and footbridges.
- Building roads, strongpoints, shelters, etc.
- Operating flamethrowers.

Experience showed that the infantry regiment's engineer platoon was too weak for the many tasks encountered in Russia.

Road-building (artwork by Uffz. Julius Nordmann). *RCT*

Waffen-SS

Reichsführer-SS Heinrich Himmler's personal army grew from a paramilitary wing of the Nazi Party to a military force of nearly 40 divisions, a number of which were created from foreign volunteers and conscripts. Firmly and directly linked to all the worst excesses of the Nazis' policies of genocide and murder, it was declared a criminal organization during the Nuremberg Trials. It was linked to atrocities against Allied soldiers as well as involvement with the SS-Einsatzgruppen in the east. Overmans puts its own death toll as 314,000.

The line-up for *Unternehmen Barbarossa* included several Waffen-SS units: in Heeresgruppe Nord—SS-Totenkopf Division (in Panzergruppe 4) and SS-Polizei Division; in Heeresgruppe Mitte—SS-Reich Division (in Panzergruppe 2); in Heeresgruppe Süd—SS-Division (mot.) Leibstandarte SS Adolf Hitler and SS-Wiking Division (both in Panzergruppe 1).

Totenkopf was decimated in the Demyansk pocket with over 13,000 casualties. Refitted as a Panzergrenadier division it took part (along with Leibstandarte and Das Reich) in the recapture of Kharkov before the battle of Kursk.

During 1942, Leibstandarte, Das Reich, Totenkopf, and Wiking became tank divisions. In 1943 Hohenstaufen and Frundsberg were formed and by October both had also been constituted as tank divisions. By the time of *Unternehmen Zitadelle* (July 5, 1943) the Waffen-SS contingent had swelled to II. SS-Panzerkorps (1. SS-Panzer-Division Leibstandarte SS Adolf Hitler, 2. SS-Panzer-Division Das Reich, and 3. SS-Panzer-Division Totenkopf). Leibstandarte sustained around 4,500 casualties during the Kursk battles and some of its veterans became the nucleus for the 12. SS-Panzer-Division Hitlerjugend. As II. Panzerkorps they fought to prevent the destruction of 1. Panzerarmee before being sent to combat the Normandy landings.

The ORBATs of the Waffen-SS tank divisions contained two panzergrenadier regiments of three battalions each. Of these, two of the six were equipped with SdKfz 251 SPWs. The other four battalions were truck borne. Unusually, *SS-Panzergrenadiere* had white *Waffenfarben* (infantry corps colors) rather than the grass green used by the German Army's *Panzergrenadiere*.

Men of the 18. SS-Freiwilligen Panzergrenadier-Division Horst Wessel involved in suppressing the Slovak National Uprising in August 1944. Note distinctive Waffen-SS camouflage. *NAC*

Two men from the Germania Regiment of 5. SS-Panzer-Division Wiking man an MG 34 on an AA tripod base in a village near Uman, Ukraine. Note the SS helmet flash and the ammunition box hanging from the tripod's central point to provide stability. *NAC*

Other Soldiers on the Eastern Front

While the bulk of infantrymen were German Army or Waffen-SS, there were other elements as well who played important roles—operating directly for the armed forces (*Wehrmachtgefolge*) and performing supply, construction, policing, and training functions. The most obvious are outlined below.

Reichsarbeitsdienst (RAD—Reich Labor Service)

A law in 1935 made service in the RAD compulsory for all young Germans. It helped to build fortifications and formed the nucleus of the construction battalions of the army and

Young men and women had no choice but to join the RAD. Although not part of the Wehrmacht, the men had six months away from home to be hardened up and learn basic military skills. Prior to being called up they worked on the land, built roads, drained swampland, and helped with the harvest along with other duties. The RAD motto was *Arbeit adelt* (work ennobles) and the organization provided a cadre of fit young men with basic military skills ready for conscription. *RCT*

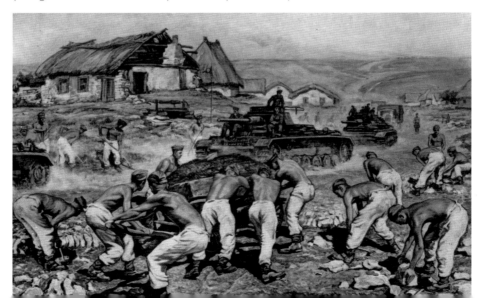

Luftwaffe at the outbreak of war, working closely with the engineers. By 1943 the RAD men were completely militarized and as well as shovel work, they were employed to lay minefields, man fortifications, and were taught antitank and antiaircraft defense. Units in parts of the front were often incorporated into the Wehrmacht without further ado.

This arm badge identifies an RAD member of *Abteilung* (section) 6 from *Gruppe* (Group) 172. *Gruppen* 170–177 were based in the *Arbeitsgau* (work district) of Niedersachsen-Mitte. *RCT*

SS Police Units

The *Ordnungspolizei* (Orpos, the Order Police) were directly involved in the Nazis' genocidal activities, working with the Einsatzgruppen. The Orpos were expanded into battalions to cope with the security, anti-partisan and -guerrilla warfare behind the lines of the swiftly advancing German forces. At times SS police units had to join combat troops on the front line, especially where defensive operations became urgent.

The orange police eagle identifies this as a *Feldgendarmerie* (Army Field Police) sleeve badge. The Feldgendarmerie was entirely separate from the Orpos. *Wiki Commons/Museonline (CC BY-SA 4.0)*

Allies

The main German allies involved in *Barbarossa* were the Finns, Hungarians, Italians, and Romanians.

The Finns, after giving the invading Soviets a bloody nose when they invaded Finland in 1939, were forced to make peace in March 1940. However, when the Soviets bombed Finnish cities three days after *Unternehmen Barbarossa* began, Finland declared war on the Axis side and allowed German troops stationed in Finland to begin offensive warfare. Thus, what the Finns know as the Continuation War began. It would end when they were forced

A member of the Ordnungspolizei carrying the distinctive Bergmann SMG. *NAC*

Hungary signed the Tripartite Pact in 1940 and invaded Yugoslavia along with Germany in 1941. Five days after *Barbarossa* began, Hungary declared war on the Soviet Union and joined the invasion. Some 300,000 Hungarian soldiers died in the fighting. This Hungarian is wearing the winter service overcoat with double cuff and rank stripe and carries an MP 40. *Fortepan (Miklós Lajos)*

to change sides and expel the Germans in September 1944 in what was the Lapland War. By that time, the Finns had sustained 225,000 casualties including 63,200 dead.

Hungary resisted joining in the war until June 26, 1941, when the Red Air Force bombed Košice. On April 11, 1942, the poorly trained Second Army joined Heeresgruppe Süd in Ukraine. Most of the field divisions were light field divisions of two infantry regiments each. The army had inadequate transport and artillery, air, and armor support, so suffered heavy casualties. It was then tasked with protecting the flank of German 6. Armee as it advanced to and fought in Stalingrad. The Hungarians were destroyed by the Soviet counteroffensives

of winter 1942–43. Fewer than 40,000 men returned to Hungary from the initial force of about 200,000 Hungarian soldiers and 50,000 Jewish forced laborers. 100,000 were dead, 35,000 wounded, and 60,000 taken prisoner.

The Italian involvement in the east was a debacle that saw the unprepared, ill-equipped Corpo di Spedizione Italiano in Russia (CSIR) sent to the Eastern Front in mid-July 1941. It was joined a year later by the Armata Italiana in Russia (ARMIR). Like the Hungarians and Romanians, it ended up protecting the flank of 6. Armee. The Russian offensive of December 16, 1942, overwhelmed II and XXXV Italian Army Corps, and the Italian divisions were

The Finns were natural allies of the Germans once *Barbarossa* began. This is a Wolf Willrich postcard of a Finnish reconnaissance squad leader. He carries a Suomi KP/-31 SMG. *RCT*

The Soldier

forced into a hasty retreat. On January 13, 1943, another offensive wiped out the Alpini and the Italian forces retreated further. Repatriation took place in March 1943. Of the 300,000 Italian troops committed, fewer than 150,000 returned to Italy, of whom 34,000 were wounded. They left behind 30,000 dead; 54,000 more died in captivity.

The Romanians fought alongside the Germans until August 1944 when a coup d'état allowed them to change sides. They then fought alongside the Red Army, sustaining nearly 160,000 casualties. Their involvement in *Barbarossa* was very similar to the other German Allies, except they were involved in larger numbers as the Romanians had 686,258 men under arms in summer 1941 and a total of 1,224,691 in the summer of 1944. They were let down by their equipment and logistics, and were decimated around Stalingrad, losing 158,854 men (dead, wounded, and missing) between November 19, 1942 and January 7, 1943.

Hiwis—*Hilfswillige* (Auxiliary Volunteers)

While some Soviet citizens detested the regime and were only too willing to join their "liberators," the majority of Hiwis made a more pragmatic decision. Locals who could see how things would go under the Germans or POWs who joined up rather than go for the very long odds of being able to survive captivity, the Hiwis were used in very large numbers on the Eastern Front. Fully 25 percent of 6. Armee in Stalingrad was composed of Hiwis. By 1944 there were 600,000 of them.

> In my division we counted about 300 or 400 of these Russians auxiliaries. They joined us during the first winter. Either they were captured soldiers or soldiers at home trying to get work. They helped in transporting wounded, they worked in the workshops and some worked as interpreters. When we went to France in December 1942, we received the strictest orders not to take those guys along. So we had a very hard time selecting those we wanted to take along because we thought of them as part of our panzer division. We took them back into the campaign in 1943–1945 … They were volunteers and they were asked to serve many times in serious spots, for instances in those periods we were under attack and in a very difficult position. I can only say that those men went with us into captivity to the U.S. armed forces in May 1945 in Austria. And then there began a very

Two former Soviet soldiers, now Hiwis in the German Army, decorated with the General Assault Badge. *Bundesarchiv 101I-004-3632-24*

difficult period because the Red Army was looking for them. So the commander of our camp told the divisional commander one evening, "Sir, I am sorry but you must get rid of your people," and he said, "I will not pass them over to the U.S." He answered, "I do not ask you. But in four days' time I must report how many auxiliaries are with you." So we informed the auxiliaries, gave them maps, and some of us went with them into the mountains and woods which was helpful at that time and they remained in Germany. And when my division meets today there come always between 30–35 of those auxiliaries who survived the war.

Osttruppen and *Ostlegionen*

While many of those who joined the Axis to fight the Red Army did so to escape captivity and almost certain death, others did so for reasons of antipathy towards the Soviet state—such as those from the Baltic states or Ukraine. The Germans pushed the religious angle to recruit from the Soviet Muslim states. From winter 1941–42 first security units—used often in anti-partisan warfare—and later military units were formed. Hitler didn't like the idea of using Slav and Turkic peoples because of the Nazi racial views, but German manpower shortages necessitated this, and so as well as the *Ostbataillone* (Eastern battalions), a range of *Ostlegionen* (Eastern legions) were formed. On December 13, 1942, the position of *Inspekteur der Osttruppen im OKH* was created, a position that was redesignated *General der Osttruppen* in early 1943, and *General der Freiwillige-Verbände* (Volunteer Troops) on January 1, 1944. It was first held by Generalleutnant Heinz Hellmich and then, from January 1944, by General der Kavallerie Ernst Köstring. On May 5, 1943 there were 10 regiments, 170 battalions, 221 companies, and 11 platoons/sections of Eastern troops.

One of the main elements was the renegade Russian Liberation Army (ROA, *Russkaia Osvoboditelnaia Armiaa*) headed by Soviet General Andrei A. Vlasov. It was these numbers (by autumn 1943 427,000 volunteers) that allowed the inspectorate to continue in the face of German anti-Vlasov elements. What did happen was that most of these volunteers were sent west rather than run the risk of them betraying the Germans in the east.

General Andrei Vlasov stands in front of one of the units of the Russian Liberation Army. A decorated Soviet general, Vlasov was captured in July 1942 and chose to turn against Stalin. In 1944 he was allowed to raise the Russian Liberation Army. At the end of the war, he was captured and executed. *NAC*

German Divisional Organization

Organization of infantry in 252. Infanterie-Division

Year	Regiment	Battalion	Total Bns
1939	3	3	9
1940	3	3	9
1941	3	3	9
1942	3	2	6
1943	2	3 + Fus Bn	7
1943 Sep	2	2 + Fus Bn	5
1944	3	2 + Fus Bn	7

In 1939 the division had the (apparently) ideal triple structure: three regiments with three battalions of three companies each (plus one MG company with three HMG platoons). As well as the infantry there were three light artillery battalions, an antitank battalion and engineer battalion, again with three companies each.

During and after the attack on Moscow a battalion in each regiment had to be disbanded. After that, the three regiments continued with two battalions each. At the beginning of 1943 headquarters and regimental units of one infantry regiment were disbanded and, with the personnel thus gained, a division fusilier battalion was set up, a considerable increase in combat strength.

After September 1943 the division had only five infantry battalions which were filled up after heavy losses at the beginning of 1944 and which had to defend a section of 30 kilometers of main line of resistance until summer 1944.

Meanwhile, it had been realized at OKH that with the current state of warfare an infantry regiment with three battalions was too ponderous. On October 2, 1943, the OKH established the *neue Art* (new style) division that became known as the Type 44. The reorganization saw the third battalion disbanded and the reconnaissance units replaced by a so-called *Fusilier Bataillon*. (This change generally led to movement of grenadier regiments between divisions.)

Therefore, in May 1944, a new regiment with two battalions was established; the division again had three regimental headquarters with two battalions each and the fusilier battalion. That structure was retained for the rest of the war.

In January 1945 the division was structured and organized as follows:

- Div HQ with two CPs but without a regular deputy commander.
- Three infantry regiments (7., 461., and 472.) essentially structured the same: HQ company with a signal platoon and an infantry engineer platoon; an antitank company with two motorized 7.5cm antitank artillery guns—although a few weeks later some of the antitank guns were pulled by horses because of a lack of fuel—and a platoon with 12 bazookas; one heavy weapons company with 2 heavy and 6 light guns; two infantry battalions with three infantry companies and an MG company each, the latter equipped with 6 HMGs, 2–3 12cm mortars and 4–5 8cm mortars; there was

The German infantry divisions often marched 40–50 kilometers a day. As they did, more and more equipment was discarded or piled up on horse-drawn wagons. *RCT*

a difference between the two "old" regiments and the regiment established in 1944; the old ones had a cavalry platoon and a heavy infantry gun platoon each, the new one did not; signal battalion including radio and telephone company, with the two teams for telephone and radio intelligence.

- Engineer battalion consisting of only two companies, one of them motorized.
- Antitank battalion consisting of a weakly staffed 7.5cm motorized antitank gun company, an incomplete 2cm antiaircraft gun company, and a company established in December 1944 equipped with 10 Hetzers (7.5cm assault guns).
- Division's fusilier battalion was excellently equipped for those days: three fusilier companies with 2 HMGs each, 2 x 8cm mortars, the heavy company with 8 x HMGs, 4 x 120mm mortars and 3 x 7.5cm antitank guns.
- Artillery regiment which had 31 light and 9 heavy field howitzers, horse drawn. Some heavy guns were towed by tractors captured in 1941.
- Field replacement battalion, medical facilities, and the supply and service regiment.

Discounting regimental HQ company, the heavy weapons and the antitank companies, the combat strength of the infantry battalions can therefore be estimated at 300 to 350 personnel. The division had one civil heavy engineer battalion, a convalescent home, and a front theater, the military personnel of which also had a military occupational specialty, and a band (in 1943 it still had four). The front theater and convalescent home were troop welfare installations which had proven their worth since 1942; the heavy engineer battalion had existed since 1943.

Regimental organization

This changed during the war. The basic organization of the battalion into three rifle companies and one heavy company remained the same, although the extent of the rifle company's heavy weapons was much debated. In 1939 it had two HMGs and three light 5cm mortars, but the HMGs were removed after the Polish campaign and the 5cm mortars were abolished because they were ineffective during the 1940 French campaign. On the Eastern Front that changed with an increase in LMGs, rifle grenade launchers, HMGs and, in the case of the panzergrenadiers, 8cm mortars.

In the 1944 regiment, machine guns were increased in number and the MG 34 was replaced, wherever possible, by the MG 42. The infantrymen would have liked an automatic rifle and they started to be issued in 1944, but there weren't enough to equip all the units. The number of mortars increased and a heavier 12cm—like the Russian version—was introduced.

For antitank defense the early-war 3.7cm and 5cm guns were soon useless. There was a lack of larger calibers although the infantrymen did have the Panzerschreck and Panzerfaust. Where possible, the infantry worked with StuGs, but they were in too short supply to dole out to the infantry regiments.

Specialized engineer units became part of infantry regiments rather than giving some infantry engineer training. Vehicles, or the lack of them, became a problem. The heavy horse-drawn vehicles which the infantry used in 1939 soon proved worthless and were replaced by light Russian farm carts in summer and, in winter, by *panje* sledges. *Panzergrenadiere* and motorized infantry moved in trucks or halftracks, but finding spare parts, tires, and fuel was problematic.

Meal break. Note the motorcyclist's rubberized waterproof *Kradmantel* overcoat. *RCT*

The SdKfz 251 was the most common of the German halftracks. Designed to transport panzergrenadiers into battle, the standard vehicle support weapon was the shielded MG 34 or MG 42. There were many variations such as the SdKfz 251/10 carrying a 3.7cm antitank gun (in background). Photo dated June 26, 1941. *NAC*

Infantry prepare for an attack. Attrition soon saw establishment numbers drop and regiments would use administrative and supply troops—even specialist troops such as combat engineers—on the front line as necessary. *NAC*

The Soviet Union quickly proved too much for the German heavy horses. They were forced to adapt and take up smaller, sturdier animals. Brauner's 1942 watercolor. *RCT*

Uniforms and Clothing

The standard Heer uniform at the start of the war was the gray-green M1936 pattern. Amongst other features it had a dark-green collar and *Waffenfarbe* (corps colors) on the shoulders. It went through various small changes over the next few years but was extensively revised with the introduction of the M1943 version—a tunic, trousers, and shirt. The M1943 uniform incorporated practical improvements and as far as possible made economies. The tunic was shorter, had six buttons in place of five, and no longer had the pocket pleats or the dark-green facings. The liners were made of synthetic silk or viscose.

The final version of the uniform was the M1944, produced with whatever materials were available. The amount of cloth used was reduced by shortening the length of the tunic. As dyes were in short supply, the colors were extremely variable. The

Diagram showing a Leutnant wearing the white Waffenfarbe of the infantry. *U.S. Army*

This panzergrenadier wears a typical equipment rig along with M43 tunic and trousers, gaiters, and ankle boots. *SF*

trousers were didn't need braces, the pockets had flaps, and the legs were designed to be used with ankle boots and gaiters.

Alongside the standard clothing, a summer uniform was produced in 1942. This was composed of a *Drillichbluse* (tunic) and matching *Drillichhosen* (trousers). Two versions were produced during the war: the first was dark green and made of linen, but as material shortages got worse, they were increasingly manufactured from synthetic substitutes which were grayer in color.

One point to remember is that a key element throughout the war was the German mix-and-match approach to keeping everything functional and working. Often what soldiers wore depended on the climate, conditions, and season. A lot of cold weather kit was made locally, and each soldier modified his kit to suit the situation and his personal preference.

Top: Officers wearing a mixture of headgear: at left an old style *Feldmütze* (the crusher), then two *Schirmmützen*, then three new style *Feldmützen*. They all wear officer's breeches and riding boots. *RCT*

Above right: Protection against insects is absolutely essential in damp and swampy areas. The protection provided was mosquito nets and gloves. *RCT*

Right: The double-breasted rubberized overcoat could be buttoned around the legs to make it easier to sit on a motorcycle. *RCT*

Winter Clothing

Winter 1941–42 came as a shock and led to improvisations of clothing:

> To alleviate the lack of adequate clothing during the winter of 1941–42, several divisions helped themselves by organizing large sewing workrooms in nearby Russian cities. From used blankets and old clothing, local workers produced flannel waistbands, earmuffs, waistcoats, footcloths, and mittens with separate thumbs and index fingers. Sheepskins were tanned and transformed into coats for sentries and a limited number of felt boots were manufactured in small Russian workshops. It was possible to requisition fur garments and felt boots from local inhabitants for a small number of men. Some winter clothing was also acquired from dead enemy soldiers. Fur-lined coats, warm underwear, gloves, and earmuffs of regular winter issue did not arrive from Germany until the early spring of 1942. During the first crucial winter the available supply was sufficient for only a small percentage of the forces. The clothing of the great majority of men was not nearly adequate since few of them had more than one item of winter clothes. Whoever possessed extra underwear wore one set on top of the other. All supplies of underclothing in the divisional and army dumps were issued. Eventually every man was able to protect his head and ears to some extent by using rags and waistbands.
>
> Effective relief gradually reached the front once the so-called fur collection campaign got under way throughout the Reich. This campaign was by far the greatest and most valuable improvisation in the field of clothing. Even though the outfits were of varied appearance they fulfilled their purpose. If it had been started earlier many casualties could have been prevented during the severe winter of 1941–42.

The *Winterhilfswerk des Deutschen Volkes* (Winter Relief of the German People)—WHW—was an annual drive to help the welfare state. It purported to be voluntary, but everyone was pressurized to contribute, often by Hitlerjugend collectors. The furs and clothing collected for the front in 1941–42 did something to help the situation, although the logistical effort of getting the clothing to the front meant that there were still many casualties.

A thorough review of winter clothing resulted in a full set of winter equipment: hooded waterproof parkas and heavy water-resistant trousers, tunic, and gloves. All were white on one side and either green camouflage or field gray on the other. These were a significant improvement, but the boots used by the Russians were still considered superior and whenever possible the German soldiers did their best to acquire them.

Collection tin from the 1941–42 *Kriegs-Winterhilfswerk des Deutschen Volkes* (War winter relief of the German people). The collectors were known as can rattlers. *Wiki Commons Drrcs15 (CC BY-SA 4.0)*

A well-known view showing the lengths soldiers went to to camouflage themselves in winter 1941–42. *Bundesarchiv 101I-268-0178-10*

These photos show a reenactor wearing the reversible winter uniforms introduced in 1942–43 (note replica Panzerschreck). *SF*

"Durch russische Steppe" (Through Russian Steppes) after Rudolf Lipus shows a squad marching through the rain, their camouflaged tent quarters covering their weapons. *RCT*

The cowhide *Tornister* (pack), with its hairy outer, became less used as the war went on. The replacement was a hard-wearing M44 rucksack. The M44s came with many variations depending on who made them. More often than not, wartime economies meant that they were made with whatever canvas came to hand, recycled, refurbished, or new. *SF*

Typical pack contents: boots, gloves, socks etc. *SF*

The soldier facing the camera wears one of the many *Windblusen*—anoraks—provided in the later years of the war. This one is notable for its three pockets on the chest. It also had a central button to allow a tailpiece to button under the crotch. To his right, the soldiers wear reversible winter uniforms introduced in 1942–43. *SF collection*

Below left and right: The problems of the first winter were caused because the supply system could not get the bulky winter equipment to the front from rear depots in Germany and Poland as ammunition and medical supplies were prioritized on the rail links. This didn't happen in the following winters, and specialist clothing was provided. These photos show a reenactor wearing a reversible mouse-gray jacket and a wartime version. *SF; RCT*

Weapons

The weapons of the infantryman on the Eastern Front changed over nearly four years of war. While many soldiers still carried machine pistols, squad LMGs, ammunition, *Stielgranaten* (stick grenades) and Kar98ks, by 1945 there were Panzerschreck and Panzerfaust, 12cm mortars, 7.5cm antitank guns, and a range of SP guns as well as a sprinkling of captured equipment. The heavier weapons in the 1941 and 1944 infantry and panzergrenadier divisions were:

Weapon	1941	1944	Panzergrenadier
MGs (LMGs on bipods; HMGs on tripods)	MG 34s	MG 34/MG 42	MG 34/MG 42
Antitank weapons	PzB 38/39 rifles; 3.7cm/5cm guns	Panzerschreck/ Panzerfaust 7.5cm/7.5cm SP gun	7.5cm/7.5cm SP guns
Mortars	Lt (5cm)/Med (8cm)	Med (8cm)/Hy (12cm)	Med (8cm)/Hy (12cm)
Inf guns	7.5cm leIG/15cm sIG33	7.5cm leIG/15cm sIG33	7.5cm/15cm SP guns
Howitzers	10.5cm leFH/15cm sFH	10.5cm leFH/15cm sFH	10.5cm leFH/15cm sFH, 10.5cm/15cm SP guns
Armor	–	–	StuG/Jagdpanzer IV
Flak guns	2cm	2cm	2cm/3.7cm/8.8cm

Nominal ammunition loads—extra rounds often carried—and each rifle company carried 140 x rifles, 90 x M24 and 120 x M39 grenades, and 36 Panzerfausts:

Weapon	Magazine	Total rounds	KAN[5]
P38 pistol	Holster held a mag; 1 mag in weapon	2 x 8-round mags = 16	16
Kar98k[1]	1911 belt pouches, 3 each on L and R	13 x 5-round clips = 65	75
SMGs[2] MP28/38/40	Ammo pouches, 3 each on L and R	7 x 32-round mags = 224	512
MP44/ StG44[3]	2 x pouches each of 3 mags	7 x 25-round mags = 175	540
LMG[4]	Gunner 1 x 50-round drum	1,150	2,500

[1] Each holding 2 clips; 1 x clip on weapon.

[2] 1 x mag on weapon.

[3] 1 x mag on weapon (restricted to 25 rounds).

[4] Assistant 4 x drums; 2 x 300-round boxes.

[5] KAN = *Kriegsausrüstungsnachweisung* = List of a unit's equipment.

The only German weapon able to kill Soviet tanks at extended ranges was the 8.8cm. However, because it was so valuable and—thanks to a high silhouette—so vulnerable, it was commonly posted well behind German forward positions. Thus hidden, the heavy flak guns were safe from suppression by Russian artillery and from early destruction by direct fire, but they could not use their extended range to blast enemy tanks far forward of the German lines. This meant that neither the lighter Paks nor the heavy 8.8cm Flak guns provided an effective standoff antitank capability. *RCT*

Weapons of the German infantry division as produced by the U.S. Army Orientation Course in 1944. It identifies: 1. Bayonet, 2. Hand grenade, 3. Pistol, 4. SMG, 5. Rifle, 6. LMG, 7. 5cmm mortar, 8. Antitank rifle, 9. HMG, 10. 8cm mortar, 11. 3.7cm antitank gun, 12. 5cm antitank gun, 13. 7.5cm light infantry gun, 14. 15cm heavy infantry gun, 15. 10.5cm light howitzer, 16. 15cm heavy howitzer, and 17. 10cm gun. *NARA*

WEAPONS of the German Infantry Division

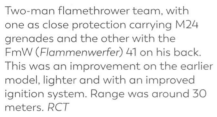

Two-man flamethrower team, with one as close protection carrying M24 grenades and the other with the FmW (*Flammenwerfer*) 41 on his back. This was an improvement on the earlier model, lighter and with an improved ignition system. Range was around 30 meters. *RCT*

Pipe-smoking Landser carrying an *Essenträger* (food carrying container) and a Kar98k carbine—the standard-issue infantryman's weapon from 1935. Shorter than its predecessor (k = *kurz* = short), it used a five-round stripper-clip top-loading 7.92mm Mauser spitzer cartridge. It had a hooded front sight blade, a laminated stock and had an open-sight range of 550 meters, farther with optics. *RCT*

The rifle grenade launcher (*Gewehrsprenggranate*) saw a high-explosive grenade slotted onto the barrel attachment (*Schießbecher*). With the butt on the ground (shoulder if necessary), the grenade was launched either by a special cartridge that fired a small wooden projectile which primed the grenade (the larger Gewehr-Panzergranate 40) or by a flash from a blank cartridge (smaller Panzergranate 30). Note the box containing 30mm high explosive grenades. This was a versatile weapon system with a range of missiles that could be used for antitank or bunker-busting. Opinions vary as to its merits. Its sighting mechanism was unsatisfactory, and its value depended mainly on the operator's training. The launcher could also be used on the *Panzerbuchse* (antitank rifle). The success of the launcher contributed to the deletion of the 5cm mortar from the rifle platoon's TO&E, and the introduction of the 8cm. *NAC*

Above left: Hitler's favorite war artist, Josef Arens, produced *Männer und Waffen des Deutschen Heeres* (*Men and Weapons of the German Army*) in 1941. This image shows an 18–70cm stereoscopic rangefinder on a tripod mount as used mainly by MG and mortar teams. (It was used with a shoulder harness in conjunction with AA MG or light Flak.) The rangefinder provided x11 magnification with an artificial infinity adjuster and came in six different sizes/widths. The larger ones worked with AA batteries, fortifications and Flak and required generators, transport vehicles and a large crew. *RCT*

Above right: The 3.7cm Pak 35/36 was the principal German antitank gun during the early years of the war. It fired HE, AP, and AP40 projectiles and a hollow-charge stick bomb (as seen in *Saving Private Ryan*). It had a range of around 400 meters. Here an Infanterie-Regiment 89 3.7cm Pak 36 gun in Kharkov during October 1941. *NAC*

Below: The 2cm Flak 30 was the original German Army Flak defense. The Flak 38 improved the rate of fire and was adopted in 1938. Later, when superseded by 3.7cm Flak guns, a 2cm Flakvierling with four Flak 38s was used. *RCT*

Left: 1. Skijäger-Brigade MG 42 machine-gun crew in Russia, January 1944. The standing man has an MP 43—a weapon that would be renamed the Sturmgewehr 44 assault rifle in March 1944. There's a story that the name change was Hitler's idea. It could be used as a submachine gun or fire single shots to a maximum range of 200 meters. It was extremely easy to field strip as it only had six parts and the upper and lower receivers hinged behind the magazine well. The weapon worked well in Russia and was less affected by dirt, cold, and snow, rarely misfired and rarely suffered from stoppages. Its only problem was that it appeared too late in the war to have a significant impact. *Bundesarchiv 101I-691-0244-11*

Center left: Both sides made great use of mines and metal detectors—the main German ones were the Wien 41 and Frankfurt 42. At Kursk the Russians laid half a million antitank and antipersonnel mines, channeling the German tanks into killing zones. Both sides positioned snipers to kill mine-clearance crews. This engineer is from 15. Infanterie-Division during the opening months of *Barbarossa. NARA*

Below left: At the start of the war the Germans had three main landmines: the Tellermine-29 and -35 antitank and anti-personnel Schützenmine-35 (S-mine). This is a Tellermine, probably a TMi-35, being laid and prepared (*Teller* = plate). Over 3.6 million were produced as they were reliable and could be used anywhere, even underwater if pre-prepared. It was ignited by pressure, 90kg on the edge and 180kg on the centre. Mines were effective as they delayed the enemy's attack, although the minefields, just like barbed-wire entanglements, could be destroyed by heavy barrages fired by Soviet artillery at the outset of an attack. A key element in German minefields was covering fire. A listening post of a couple of men on the rearward edge could alert a covering party equipped with LMGs to ensure enemy who strayed into the minefield paid the price. This soldier is either a Gebirgsjäger or Skijäger and wears a reversible camouflaged/white overall. He also wears ski boots with their squared front, soles, and lacing hooks. *SF collection*

Obergefreiter Fritz Brauner's watercolor shows a winter defensive position with the 8cm mortar about to fire. Note the spacing between the mortar and the gun team to the left of the painting. The GrW 34 had a good reputation for reliability and accuracy and was man-portable, just, with special harnesses for the barrel, bipod, and baseplate. Once set up and ready, the bomb was dropped down the tube and fired when it hit the fixed firing-pin. Ten or 12 rounds could be fired in a minute, with a maximum range of 2,400 meters with propelling charge 4. The propellant looked like an 8cm split penny washer and went around the stem of the round by the tailfins. Mortars proved an outstanding success in the Russian campaign. Along with the automatic rifle, they proved to be the main infantry weapons of the period. Both German 8cm and 12cm models were excellent, although the smaller-caliber 5cm wasn't worth the ammunition expenditure. *RCT*

To the infantryman the hand grenade is indispensable— it's the high-angle weapon for close combat. The M24 stick grenade was the main offensive weapon. The egg-shaped M39—easier to throw but with a small filling—with a fragmentation sleeve was a good defensive option. A Willrich image. *RCT*

The Panzerfaust Pzf 30 (gross)—where *gross* = large—was a man-portable, recoilless, disposable tube to kill tanks. The shaped/hollow charge had a range of about 50 meters depending on the model. About 8 million of all types were produced. It wasn't healthy to fire from an enclosed area, but by the end of the war anyone who could hold it had been trained to fire it. Its short range was its biggest drawback. The MP 40 SMG was simple to manufacture using stamped steel. Rate of fire was 500–550 rounds/ minute from a 32-round magazine. *NARA*

Transport and Services

The immensity of the Soviet Union and its extremes of weather and terrain all militate against an invader. The farther the German front line advanced from the border, the greater the need for good supplies and good logistics.

The Germans would have liked to use the railways but couldn't do so immediately because the Soviet rail and loading gauges were different to the German equivalents and because the Soviets had effectively rescued most of the stock and motive power while sabotaging the infrastructure. They would have liked to use large numbers of trucks but motor transport was always a problem for the German Army whose dependence on horses to pull not only supply wagons but also artillery caused immeasurable difficulties. Trucks need rubber for tires and fuel to run: both commodities were in short supply for Germany which had no home production capability for either. As the infantry hastened—mainly on foot—to succeed where Napoleon's great army hadn't, and as autumn muds gave way to frost, there would have been many wondering what would happen when the snows came. When they did, the failures of the German logistical machine became clear.

Barbarossa had been predicated on a successful and swift Blitzkrieg, a short war that kicked the Soviet door in and watched as Stalin and his government toppled. Militarily, that's pretty much exactly what happened: the Soviets couldn't stop the Axis forces whose complete air superiority rammed home their military superiority. But crucially the government didn't fall. Russia didn't fragment but coalesced against the invaders. As the weather changed, as men and horses died of cold and exposure, the short-term planning saw the men at the front lack winter clothing and the knowledge of how to fight in the extreme conditions. Much of the equipment the men at the front needed was sitting in warehouses without the wherewithal to get to them.

Getting equipment, fuel, food, or anything to the front line was a problem. By August 1941 the number of working trucks in the logistical network had dropped below 60 percent. But *Unternehmen Barbarossa* didn't fail because of transport and supply problems. The soldiers on the ground improvised brilliantly and by 1942 most of the cold weather issues had been rectified. However, the breathing space allowed the Soviets to shore up their own production and supply position and live to continue the battle.

A typical German artillery column with horse-drawn 10.5cm leFH18 howitzers. Many of these howitzers bogged down and had to be abandoned in the retreat from Moscow. The later 18/40 used the lighter Pak 40 trail and wider wheels. *NAC*

Horse-drawn carts head for Stalingrad. The lucky ones—some 17,000—got out a week before Operation *Uranus* encircled 6. Armee. GFM Friedrich Paulus ordered them to leave because the Luftwaffe wasn't meeting its supply deliveries. Over 12,000 horses ended up being eaten. *SF collection*

Corduroy Roads

Where roads or tracks didn't exist, corduroy roads had to be constructed. The main element was the abundant timber from the vast Russian forests. As seen in the photo, layers of cut wood were laid and bound with wire and filled with anything available—sand, brushwood, rubble, or cinders. Major Richert, Operations Officer of 134. Infanterie-Division, wrote in a report of September–October 1942:

> We were back in the woods again. The division at once readied its positions and built corduroy roads for two-way traffic. However tiring it was at first for men and horses to move over such roads, they later facilitated all transportation problems in a most decisive manner. ... At the beginning of October motor vehicle traffic was stopped until about the middle of November, and traffic was only possible on the corduroy roads. These had been partly ballasted with gravel taken from a nearby pit and distributed by horse-drawn columns. Even on these roads only light traffic was permitted, and it was strictly controlled sectionally. Until the ground was sufficiently frozen, traffic beyond the corduroy section was confined to the evacuation of casualties and the transport of bread and fresh meat. In contrast to the autumn mud period of the previous year everything had been well prepared for the winter, including the distribution and storage of grain and hay in sufficient quantity for the large number of horses attached to the division. Again, the horses had proved their great importance. Without them the corduroy roads could not have been built.

Supplies are loaded onto wagons at a railhead. Note the wooden road in foreground and Soviet markings on the *teplushka* (railway wagon). *RCT*

On the March

The infantry did a lot of marching. There were limited numbers of motorized infantry carried in trucks and halftracks but most were on foot with horses to drag heavy weapons. They often marched 45–50 kilometers in a day on the attack. All veteran accounts talk of their tiredness, of sores from blisters and chafing, and of the hope that the Soviets would make a stand because the adrenaline rush would make them forget their own pain. German Army manuals advised:

> On the march and in combat the following practices should be observed. Use breaks in the march and rest periods to exchange unserviceable articles of clothing and to make minor repairs. Garments left behind by wounded men should be collected and turned in without exception. In snowstorms wear the fur coat inside out and wrap a shelter half around it if it does not conflict with camouflage requirements.
>
> Particular attention should be devoted to drying wet clothes and, above all, footgear. Do not let boots or shoes dry near a fire or burning stove, because, in addition to the danger that they may burn, they may become hard and brittle. Wet footgear should be stuffed with straw or paper.
>
> Snow is an enemy of leather, and the best protection is to keep the leather soft. Care of the footgear is especially important in preparing for a march. The uppers should be greased daily, preferably when damp. Leather which has been greased too much, however, chills the feet and permits water to seep through. This treatment should not be applied just before marches, but well in advance.

Kharkov, 1941: Infanterie-Regiment 15 *Troß* (baggage train) column with horse-drawn carts. *NARA*

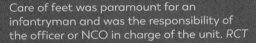

Care of feet was paramount for an infantryman and was the responsibility of the officer or NCO in charge of the unit. *RCT*

Knackered. Infantrymen—even without their packs—carry heavy kit; here hand grenades, ammo boxes, and an MG 34. They sleep when they can. *NAC*

Even in light order, rushing to the next *Kesselschlacht* (encirclement battle) was dirty and tiring. *NAC*

In extreme conditions it was very difficult to start engines as lubricants froze, so many different engine covers were used. The two vehicles from the left are Krupp Protze Kfz 70s, one with snow chains. *Fortepan (Fortepan)*

As the Germans had little strategic airpower, Soviet industry was safely out of harm's way and was able to outperform Germany's own arms production. One of the reasons for this was the large range of weapons used by German armed forces—each requiring its own spare parts, ammunition, and user skills. This table shows the numbers of weapon types in production in the Soviet Union and Germany before (A) and after (B) Speer's reorganization of German industry and highlights some of the supply difficulties that the German Army faced.

	Germany		USSR
	(A)	(B)	
Artillery	26	8	5
Antitank guns	12	1	2
Antiaircraft guns	10	2	3
Tanks, armored vehicles	18	7	6
Aircraft	42	5	18

Standardization is still a keyword in military planning. As this table shows, the Germans came to it late—and the problems were exacerbated by the use of *Beutewaffen* (booty weapons—materiel taken from subjugated countries). While the weapons—often excellent equipment—went mainly to the Ersatzheer, or coastal defense in the case of the artillery, *Barbarossa* saw large numbers of foreign vehicles in service. Liedtke suggests nearly 5,000 Renault UE Chenillette tracked vehicles and at least 13,000 French trucks meant that "40 of the 151 divisions assigned to 'Barbarossa' were equipped with captured vehicles"—this was on top of "an unknown percentage of the truck fleet belonging to the army's vital supply services" also being of foreign design. These contributed to some 2,000 different types of vehicle—a spare parts nightmare. In the short term, these vehicles were vital but after the Axis failed to achieve its aim of a short war, the road haulage fleet—and its maintenance—proved to be a continuing nightmare. Leidtke highlights the difficulties:

> Between June 1941 and the end of June 1942, the Wehrmacht had lost at least 127,731 motor vehicles and even larger numbers were in various stages of disrepair. On 20 February 1942 Heeresgruppe Süd reported that it had suffered the Totalausfälle of 23,526 of its motor vehicles since the start of operations in the East: even more disconcertingly, out of the 86,757 it still possessed, some 70,969 (81%) were not operational because they required some kind of significant overhaul or repair.

The German supply chain required trucks to take supplies from dumps at the railheads to the front. They couldn't do that if they weren't working, or the roads were impassable—and the railheads needed to be as close to fronts as possible.

Railways

When Western sources discuss German use of railways in the Soviet Union during World War II, they tell a story of a struggle to overcome technical difficulties posed by a ramshackle, old-fashioned, and low-capacity Soviet railway network. However, Russian sources tell a different story: of a highly successful system that prewar carried almost as much freight as the United States and accomplished this using a rolling stock fleet and length of track only a little larger than that of the prewar Reichsbahn. The USSR had some of the most intensively used track in the world: in 1930 it had 1,738,000 ton-km per km—130,000 more than that of the United States. (1,608,000).

The Soviet achievement was well known because they touted the success of the railways as one of the great achievements of socialism. On top of this, Germany had been a key manufacturer of locomotives for the Soviet Union: orders for 700 E Class engines—the mainstay of Soviet freight well into the 1950s—had been placed with 22 German manufacturers in 1922.

As Davie says, history shows that the key to a successful railway service in time of war is that:

> railwaymen were left to run the railways free from military interference. Military abuses included abandoning schedules, forwarding supplies before they were needed, failing to unload trains upon arrival, using rolling stock and sidings as mobile warehouses and offices (so reducing capacity and blocking tracks), and commandeering trains.

The Nazis, of course, with their overlapping jurisdictions, political infighting, and complete lack of belief in the abilities of the Slav *Untermenschen*, were never going to get the best from the Soviet railways. Part of the problem was perception. It was immediately obvious that the Russian 5ft gauge—chosen before Europe had standardized on 4ft 8.75in—meant that regauging was necessary between the two countries. Even then, the more generous Soviet loading gauge still rendered compatibility problematic.

German planning for the invasion of the Soviet Union had two major difficulties for the Reichsbahn: first, *Barbarossa* was being launched from the east—from Poland, an area that had been under Soviet control since 1939 and whose lines had been regauged to 5ft; second, that one of the anticipated decisive encirclement battles—Smolensk—was beyond the range of motor vehicles from German mobilization depots. The first led to the Otto program upgrade of the Polish railway network. The second saw civilian heavy truck/trailer combinations mobilized, mainly from the Reichsbahn's haulage company Schenker and the Nationalsozialistisches Kraftfahrkorps (National Socialist Transport Corps, or NSKK). *Eisenbahnpioniere* (railway engineers) would regauge the railways in Soviet-occupied eastern Poland with a double-track line of at least 24 train pairs a day for each *Heeresgruppe*. Additionally:

> A *Versorgungsbezirk* (supply district) would be established at a depth of 400km, in the case of Heeresgruppe Mitte at Minsk, which would be built up by moving the depots forward from the Polish border by railway.

German *Keil und Kessel* (wedge and pocket) tactics involved large pincer movements that bottled up the enemy in a *Kessel*—cauldron—and allowed the German infantry to destroy the pocket. This meant that German advances—and this was particularly true in the vast Soviet Union—often outran the railways. To bridge the gap, from August 1939 supply of the armies from the railheads was assigned to an OKH department of the *Generalquartiermeister* under Generalmajor Eduard Wagner, while the railways themselves came under the OKW department of the *Chef des Transportwesens* (chief of transport) under Generalmajor Rudolf Gercke. For *Barbarossa* Gercke formed *Feldeisenbahn-Direktion* (Field Railway Directions or FEDs) units—one for each Heeresgruppe—from railwaymen under military officers. The rear area of the armies was to be kept very narrow, as little as 200km behind the front line, with Reichskommissariate set up to administer and exploit the captured territories. In this area the Reichsverkehrsministerium (Ministry of Transport) was to set up new operating companies or *Haupteisenbahndirektion* (Main Railway Directions or HBDs) using Reichsbahn staff. Both the FEDs and HBDs were set up in mid-1941, and were short of staff, lacking equipment and totally without experience. Take the HBD Mitte set up in Brest-Litovsk as an example. It had only 60 men, too few qualified officials and little equipment—for example, none of the telephones needed to run the railway:

> There were no route maps, timetables, or station information so that locomotives had to be sent out for several days in each direction to explore the network. In September the SS shot the entire printing staff of the HBD as part of a Jewish pogrom.

The Germans had hoped that the speed of their advance would enable them to take control of the Soviet rail system in a relatively unharmed state. Nothing could be further from the truth. As they retreated from the German thrusts in 1941–42, the Soviets achieved a signal victory that is all too often unreported. The NKPS (People's Commissariat of Means of Communication) evacuated locomotives before they could fall into the hands of the Germans, in total losing less than 15 percent of the fleet of locomotives despite losing around 40 percent of the network. They were able to evacuate millions of citizens, move the war industries safely beyond the Urals and bring to the front new divisions raised in the depths of Asian Russia, something that helped save Moscow. For the rest of the war, Soviet forces were able to rely on rail transport in a way the Germans never could.

Armored trains were used by both sides throughout the Eastern Front, for example by the Germans in anti-partisan operations around Bryansk. The Germans found them so useful that they looked to increase their numbers substantially in 1944. However, loss of the steel mills in the Ukraine meant few were completed. They also impressed into service any they captured—as here. *NARA*

More importantly to the Germans, the Soviets destroyed the railway infrastructure. While the *Eisenbahnpioniere* (railway engineers) performed manfully—15,000 kilometers of track converted by December 1941; 21,000 kilometers by May 1942—they couldn't rebuild the infrastructure. The crisis came during the first winter, 1941–42, when the lack of covered locomotive depots saw many engines seize up: by February 1942, some 70 percent were unserviceable. This meant that ammunition, fuel, and fodder were more important than winter clothing. The response was to send more locos and rolling stock from Germany. This alleviated the situation on the Eastern Front but within the Reich, German manufacturing couldn't get its raw materials—particularly fuel, mainly coal—and output dropped. Armaments factories were shut down. Hitler acted. The Heer lost control of the railways, and the RVM and Organization Todt started the Ostbau 42 program, but it was too little, too late and the German Army in the east always suffered from lack of railway carrying capability. Take Stalingrad as an example. On October 20 only 12 trains reached AOK.6 carrying 5,400 tonnes. Elsewhere, the situation was also difficult. On the same day Hungarian AOK.2 was supplied by seven trains, Italian AOK.8 by four, and AOK.2 by eight. Resupply was so poor that 6. Armee sent its horses back from Stalingrad to Rostov; this cut demand for fodder but effectively immobilized the army for the winter. Indeed, in June 1944, as Operation *Bagration* began, Heeresgruppe Mitte couldn't carry both munitions and reinforcements, and had to choose between the two. Partisan sabotage also impacted German rail transport although never to huge effect.

Railways were a crucial element of the war in the east, not least because of the distances involved. The Soviets realized this and ensured that, where possible, offensives followed railway tracks as much as the terrain. The Soviet railway system was substantially better than the Germans credited, and the Soviets were also very capable of restoring destroyed bridges and lines to aid resupply to the quick-moving advances of 1944 and 1945.

One cannot overemphasize the importance of the railways in the Soviet Union. The German supply system was predicated on moving supplies from Germany and the west through to railheads, from where road or horse-drawn vehicles would supply the troops. The farther away an advance was from railway or railhead, the more difficult supplying ammunition, fodder and food became, as did returning equipment for repair to depots or the wounded to hospitals. Damage to the rail system caused serious problems to the Germans. Rails could be repaired quickly, but the Soviet railwaymen destroyed infrastructure and, more importantly, ensured that locos and rolling stock were kept out of German hands. *SF collection*

A Horse-drawn Army

In 1939, a 1st wave infantry division officially had 17,734 officers and men. Its heavy equipment included 48 artillery pieces (12 x 15cm and 36 x 10.5cm guns). Its inventory included 615 trucks and 919 horse-drawn vehicles, of which 588 were allocated to the 3 infantry regiments; the divisional artillery had 240. The division's total requirement of horses was 4,842 horses. The reserve for these horses comprised 35 cavalry mounts and 80 light and 15 heavy draft horses—130 in total.

As this divisional example shows, the German Army had a lot of horses—between 1938 and 1939 they mobilized at least 400,000. By 1939—including horses taken in the Anschluß (taking over Austria) and Czechoslovakia—the Germans had 590,000 horses. Poland offered another opportunity for acquiring horses after its surrender: 4,000 a week in April 1940. Next came the animals swept up when Holland, Belgium, and France fell to the advancing German Army. These countries specialized in heavier breeds, better for artillery and heavier haulage. By June 1941 the army in the east had assembled 625,000 horses.

These horses required a lot of looking after and at least 6 kilograms of feed a day. This was the basic minimum. Large draft horses could consume up to 9 kilograms a day or needed about eight hours grazing on grass, assuming that was available. All this added up to a remarkable 4,500 tonnes of feed required per day by the armies readied for *Barbarossa*. And as the German Army drove deeper into Russia many of its vehicles broke down and could not be replaced, so it became steadily less motorized and more dependent on its horses. The dependence on horses meant large numbers of Russians escaped encirclement or fought their way out of pockets because the infantry couldn't tighten quickly enough the net thrown round by the panzers.

Fodder began to be a real problem too and lack of food affected the horses as badly as could be expected. The oats ration in 1941 was 5 kilograms for cavalry mounts and light draft horses, 6.5 kilograms for heavy draft horses. The rapid advances led to no time to collect and distribute forage (only when the front stabilized in 1942 could this improve). Winter made the situation worse, and forage was always seen as being of lesser importance than ammunition. Its procurement in only minimum quantities resulted in an enormous loss of horses.

The problems weren't limited to the amount of feed provided. It was found that the cotton feedbags used wore out quickly. Improvisation

"A street near Kharkov," an image from Ernst Eigener's *Mein Skizzenbuch (My sketchbook)*. RCT

Zone of the interior	Army Group	Army	Division
Veterinary hospitals. Remount depots. Veterinary depots.	One or two army group veterinary hospitals.	**Installations:** Two army veterinary hospitals, partially motorised; one army veterinary park, motorised; two horse transport columns, motorised – one horse transport company as of autumn 1943; one army remount depot; one or two mobile veterinary test stations, motorised. **Army veterinary clinics:** Organisation similar but larger than veterinary company, without supply section but with horse transport motor trucks. Authorised capacity of 550 horses but often increased in the east to 2,000 or 3,000 horses; reinforced by voluntary auxiliaries and POWs. During advance, hospitals moved forward alternately; during combat or position warfare see below. **Army remount depot:** Authorised capacity of 500 remounts, usually many more; supplemented from the zone of the interior, recuperated horses from hospitals and captured horses. **Army veterinary depots:** Although motorised is dependent on rail transportation because of 500 tons of equipment including medical and dressing equipment, instruments, horseshoeing equipment, cleats and gas protective equipment. **Veterinary test stations:** Well-equipped mobile laboratory for all bacteriological, serological and chemical testing. Tests foods of animal origin from the butcher companies, tests fodder, and systematically tests all army horses for glanders. **Horse transport column or horse transport company:** For employment see below.	Authorised one veterinary company per infantry, mountain, or Luftwaffe field division, and two veterinary companies per cavalry division. **Veterinary company until 1943:** 233 men, two horse-drawn and six motorised transport vehicles. **Organisation:** One command section, one collecting section, one hospital section, one supply section, one rations section. **Equipment:** Excellently equipped with instruments, x-ray machines, and portable motor-driven dynamos. **Mission:** Transfer sick and injured horses from combat areas; treat simple cases in hospital section; for others see below. Advances with the supply forces. Assigned to the administrative forces and not to veterinary units, but received technical instructions from the latter and were commanded by veterinary officers. **Butcher company:** One per division, 50 men; provided fresh meat and sausages for 19,200 men; protected the unit against trichina and bladder worms.

A U.S. Army diagram showing the veterinary services in the German Army.

The ubiquitous horse-drawn *panje* wagon (Magyar/Hungarian for horse) was, with all its variations including sledges, the main form of transport during the long winter months and when the terrain turned to mud. Generalleutnant Hellmuth Reinhardt said: "The Russian farm cart (the German term is *Panjewagen*) is generally considered the only really efficient horse-drawn vehicle. The two-horse farm cart may even be preferable to the Russian army vehicle which uses three or four horses. The light two-horse vehicle is best suited to cross any terrain. The load should not exceed 0.4 tons to at most 0.5 tons since experience in Russia revealed the normal load capacity of each draft horse (exclusive of the vehicle's own weight) to be only about 0.2 to 0.25 tons." *RCT*

saw a wooden trough to serve three horses developed but this had the drawback of contributing to the spread of contagious diseases. During the 1941 winter German Army horse losses were running at 1,000 a day. Great use was made of Russian panje horses, but it was still important to find shelter from the cold for the horses. Mange became a problem: veterinary hospitals were swamped and having to treat more than four times the numbers expected with figures of 2,000–3,000 at a time not unusual. By November 1941, horse losses totaled 102,910 killed and 33,000 sick or unfit. The army lost 180,000 horses in winter 1941 but they kept proving their worth. Between 1940 and 1943 the German Army requisitioned 1.2 million horses from Germany and the occupied territories. They lost 1.5 million.

The 1944 division had a theoretical strength of 12,772 officers and men (a big reduction on the 17,734 of 1939). Its artillery had also been cut back to 30 x 10.5cm (originally 36) and 9 x 15cm (originally 12) guns. Truck numbers were substantially reduced to 370 (from 615). Horse numbers dropped to 3,177 (from 4,842). However, horse-drawn vehicles had increased from 919 to 1,375.

The German Army requisitioned over 400,000 horses in 1944 but that wouldn't have covered the losses that Heeresgruppe Mitte suffered in late June 1944: 35 divisions were lost and, assuming even averaging 2,000 horses in each division, it meant a loss of 70,000 horses. Replacements and requisitions ensured that on February 1, 1945, the Wehrmacht had 1,198,724 horses.

Towards the end of 1944 the veterinary companies of the infantry divisions were combined with the administrative and medical services into the administrative battalions of the new supply regiments, a measure occasioned by the shortage of personnel and motor vehicles. The veterinary officers so moved may have been better placed within a service unit than a line company, for they were largely reservists with little general military knowledge or training.

Stalingrad

The Soviet Operation *Uranus* encircled German 6. Armee by November 23, 1942. The surrounded forces held out until the end of January/early February by which time German casualties were 147,200 killed and wounded and 91,000 captured. *Die Wehrmacht* magazine of February 1943 ran several stories on Stalingrad including this one by Unteroffizier Hans U from Upper Bavaria, holder of both Iron Crosses:

> We knew already that the army had been surrounded and I found myself with my unit in the wreckage of the Dzerzhinsky Tractor Factory in the northern part of Stalingrad. Little of the factory remained other than broken walls and twisted iron bars. The Soviets hadn't tried a major attack. Then, one day three forward observation officers came to us. Two were wounded and they gave us to understand that the enemy was about to attack.
>
> The platoon to which my unit belonged was partly manned by soldiers from the supply train for whom this attack would be their first. A rifle platoon was advanced ahead of us to protect us. This unit that we hadn't seen before marched gently forward. As they waited for orders, they came under heavy fire. I immediately sent runners back to the company HQ to let the OC know what was going on. The first came back wounded. I never saw anything of the other again. A runner from the rifle platoon must have got through because towards midday there was a counterattack with two tanks and a StuG. By about 15:00 the enemy was pushed back, and we could set up a blocking position. We had even surrounded a group of about 150 men, who tried to break through the cordon with a fearsome "Hurra"; however, despite the shouting, the attempt failed miserably. Soon after, however, two battalions of Soviets appeared to break through our switch position [a defensive setup that is oblique to the front, designed to prevent hostile penetrations from being exploited to the flanks]. The StuG fought heroically and hunted Soviet tanks despite the impossible terrain and the rubble until it was knocked out.
>
> Our victuals were naturally rationed after the army was surrounded. Bread was very scarce, and horsemeat was our main food. Air supply missions tried to give us the most important commodities—above all ammunition—but few of the airdropped containers survived impact with the frozen ground.
>
> The enemy attacked every dawn and dusk. At times they were only 20 meters away, but despite the proximity they used mortars, antitank guns, and rifles. I need hardly say how fighting against such weapons at such a short range went and what demands have been made of our men as Luftwaffe air superiority slipped away and the Red Air Force became dominant.

The improvement in numbers, however, didn't improve the strategic position, but they made Hitler confident enough to attack at Kursk when he should, perhaps, have improved his defenses. Failure there—and the subsequent losses in the Soviet counteroffensive—meant that Germany was on the back foot and the Soviets never lost the initiative. The personnel and material problems would get worse, but there was one benefit to retreat: it made the lines of communication shorter and improved logistic distances. The Ostheer was able to withstand continuing and heavy attacks through the whole of 1944: the Dnieper–Carpathian offensive (December 24, 1943–May 6, 1944) cost over 250,000 and possibly as high as 380,000 casualties. It was the first of what the Russians named Stalin's "Ten Blows" that saw the Ostheer battered as Leningrad, Ukraine and the Crimea, Poland, the Baltic states, Budapest, and Belgrade were liberated, and the Red Army stood on the borders of Germany itself.

As time went on and losses escalated, the final desperate attempt to put men in the way of the Red Army saw the Nazis create the Volkssturm and call to the colors anyone aged between 16 and 60 not already serving. When these new troops, having received what training and equipment was available, reached the combat zone, the results were predicable—particularly as head of the Replacement Army, Reichsführer-SS Heinrich Himmler controlled the organization. On January 28, 1945, Hitler had to issue this order:

> The experiences in the East show that Volkssturm … units used independently have only very little fighting strength and can be smashed quickly. The fighting strength of these units, which are usually strong in numbers but insufficiently armed for modern fighting, is incomparably higher when they are used within the framework of the field army. I therefore order that when Volkssturm units as well as troops of the field army are available in a combat sector, mixed combat groups [brigades] are to be set up under unified command, so as to give support and backbone to the Volkssturm units.

Some units—mostly those defending the fortresses—fought hard and well; others collapsed and disintegrated without a fight. The 3/115 Siemensstadt Bataillon in Berlin won 26 Iron Crosses for its part in the defense of the city.

The continuing losses and use of reserves and replacements should have affected combat efficiency, but the German Army proved adaptable and resilient, often throwing together ad hoc units to form a Kampfgruppe whose sum was more than its parts. Front-line units attempted to keep back a small, well-rested assault detachment by withdrawing a small number of soldiers from the thick of the fighting to give them rest behind the lines. Before June 6, 1944, units that required rehabilitation were withdrawn and sent to recuperate in France, something that wasn't possible after the battle of Normandy and the Allies' swift advance on the Westwall.

Every male between 16 and 60 not engaged in war work had to join the *Volkssturm*. Armbands identified them. *United States Holocaust Memorial Museum Collection, Gift of Bernard Feingold*

Communications

Military communications have various levels from international-range command nets to short-range tactical nets for tankers or infantrymen. The German long-range systems allowed Hitler to maintain his close control over military action right till the end. For example, after Heeresgruppe Nord was isolated in the Courland pocket, communication with the Führer (some 300 kilometers away in Rastenburg) was maintained by land and sea cable over the approximately 4,500-kilometer route: Rastenburg–Berlin–Hamburg–Denmark–Oslo–Narvik–Petsamo–Rovaniemi–Helsinki–Reval–Riga.

There were, of course, many other methods of military communication in World War II: messengers in cars, horses, bicycles, motorcycles, or just as runners; telegraph; signal light or blinker; pyrotechnics: rockets, Very lights, flares; flags and panels (often best to communicate with aircraft); alarms: sirens, bells, and gongs were often used to warn of gas or hostile aircraft; animals—pigeons needed three days to orient, but were useful under heavy fire, flying at about a kilometer in a minute, and dogs; and the two main methods, telephone and radio.

The problem with telephone is that installation takes time and materiel. Wire is also sensitive to fire, wind, snow, frost, and storms. The enemy could also easily listen in on conversations, particularly over single-wire connections; in the danger zone, therefore, double lines and heavily insulated wires were used.

Radio became indispensable during the war, although it was also sensitive to electric storms, static, other radio transmission on similar wavelengths, mountains, and other interferences. While some of the radio traffic was decoded by Allied intelligence—Ultra certainly helped the Western Allies win their part of the war—this had no effect on the Eastern Front.

Tactically, air support, contact with artillery batteries and panzer units, command and control of units on the ground—all demanded good communications. In defense or attack—particularly the highly mobile Blitzkrieg—German communication systems were good. In defense, wire was the mainstay with junior units laying wires to their seniors. Battlefield

The Henschel Hs 126 two-seater—pilot and gunner—was an observation and liaison aircraft with short takeoff and landing capability as well as a low stalling speed. This was a practical way to take important messages to senior officers or extract a casualty.
SF collection

wire, however, could easily be broken, not only by bombardment or even bad weather but by partisan action, which was a real threat.

A battalion signals platoon had two light telephone teams in 1939 (with 10 kilometers of wire, six handsets, and a switchboard). This increased to three in 1944 with a corresponding increase in wire and handsets. Divisions had a full battalion organized with two full companies, one radio, and one telephone.

As well as wire the Ostheer made great use of radios (*Feldfunksprecher*) but were very aware of interception and the intelligence that could be gained so radio operators were taught to use radios sparingly so as not to give locations away. Once an attack was launched or a defensive battle started, short-range communications with other troops—especially mortars or artillery—was by *Feldfunksprecher* (*FeldFu*).

There were various types of radio. For short-range use, the *FeldFu* b/b1/b2 had a range of about 1,000–1,200 meters. It weighed around 2 kilograms. For medium range, the bigger *Tornisterfunkgerät* (*TornFu*) was also portable, weighed at least 20 kilograms, and could be carried by one man, although two was more common. The *TornFu* had a range of 5 to 25 kilometers (3–15 miles). Messenger dogs, carrier pigeons, and rockets (visual or sound) were used to supplement the two basic methods of radio and wire.

A signaler's trade badge was worn on the upper left sleeve. This one is red for artillery.

A *Fernsprechtrupp*—telephone section—with the man on right using a *Fernsprechtornister* (telephone pack). There were three types. Nos. 1 and 3 contained a spare battery, three reels with 500 meters of light field cable, a crank for a cable reel, headphones, a spool of earthing wire, two cable placement rods, a fork for a cable placement rod, an insert for a cable placement fork, a cable winder with crank (*Abspuler*), a battery tester in a pouch, a cable glove, a microphone, a *Zeltbahn* (camouflaged canvas that could form a tent when mated with others or act as a waterproof camouflaged poncho) , and a tin of wire connectors. The No. 2 backpack had some changes: two reels with 500 meters of light field cable and a collapsed empty reel. *U.S. Army*

The *Feldfernsprecher* (FF) 33 was developed in the 1930s with a moulded Bakelite housing, on top of which are two squares. One (at left) was a writing tab; the other was an alphabet tag. To work, all that was needed was two telephones powered by two 1.5V batteries and connected by two wires. Ranges were 3–12km for light/heavy cable on the ground and 10–60km when the line was suspended high. Double-line heavy cable had a range of 30–40km. The pouch in the foreground is for a *Kopffernhörer* 33 headphone which helped in noisy environments. *SF collection*

During World War II, radio communications were often hampered by lack of batteries. The answer was a pedal generator, as used here in the Balkans by a Gebirgsjäger unit. *NARA*

Signals unit checking line. Note the *Drahtgabel*—cable fork—at left used to guide the wire into position. The man on the pole is using climbing irons but not a climbing belt (a sketch by Arens). *RCT*

Left: Germans setting up a *TornFu b* field radio in Karelia, Finland, May 15, 1942. Note the FF33 field telephone and high rod antenna. *Finnish Archives (SA-Kuva)*

Below left: The *Torn Eb* was produced in large numbers from its introduction in 1935. It was used as a general-purpose field receiver and as an accompanying receiver for several transmitters of the type normally found installed in signals trucks (a sketch by Arens). *RCT*

Below: The *Feldfunksprecher* series (b, b1, b2, c, f, and h, and *Kleinfunksprecher* d) was used for tactical communication between battalions and companies while stationary or on the move. The f was developed as a panzergrenadier portable radio to communicate with the tanks they were supporting. This is the *FeldFu c* which had a two-part antenna, with a shorter bottom rod and a whip top section. *Bundesarchiv*

Service Troops

They don't have the charisma of the front-line infantry in any army and all too often their numbers are criticized by those who pull the strings, but without the "tail" there would be no cutting edge. The service troops provided supplies—food, fuel, ammunition, clothing—medical and veterinarian aid; they maintained vehicles, handled admin and post—always one of the key elements in boosting morale. As manpower became an issue, there were many trawls through the service troops looking to push more people onto the front line. Most of these tended to look at Armee or Heeresgruppe level, but at divisional German level too the service element was curtailed during the war. The main service elements of an infantry division included the following, the size depending on the level of motorization:

Nachschubtruppen (divisional supply troops)
Verwaltungstruppen (administrative troops)
Feldpostamt (field post office)
Kraftfahrparktruppen (motor maintenance troops).
Feldgendarmerietrupp (MP detachment)
Sanitätstruppen (medical troops)
Veterinärtruppen (veterinary troops)

During the war there were changes to the service units with some centralization. The 1944 infantry battalions in Volksgrenadier divisions had supply platoons instead of the traditional battalion and company trains, working with a divisional supply regiment.

The composition of the supply troops changed in each of the iterations of the infantry division. The man in charge of a division's service and supply troops was the *Divisions-*

Below left: The Nazis were contemptuous of Christianity. This left the German Army chaplains in a difficult position. During World War I there had been 2,000 of them; in 1939–45 half that number, and none in the Waffen-SS or Luftwaffe. After 1942, the numbers dropped as no new chaplains were appointed and those that died, fell ill or became POWs weren't replaced. In spite of this, the presence of the chaplains at the sites of mass killings helped foster the illusion that the German soldiers were still decent people. *RCT*

Below right: The gorget on a chain identifies the Feldgendarmerie when on duty. Loathed by the rank and file, they were often referred to as "chained dogs." They were responsible for traffic control, setting up holding points for enemy stragglers, and securing suspected partisans. *NARA*

Nachschubführer. His title was changed in October 1942 to *Kommandeur der Infanterie-Divisions-Nachschubtruppen*. Nafziger identifies 1. Infanterie-Division's supply troops in May 1941, just before *Unternehmen Barbarossa*, as:

1. Divisional Supply Troops
1/, 2/, 3/1. (mot.) Lt Supply Columns
4/, 5/, 6/1. (horse-drawn) Supply
    Columns
7/, 8, 9/1. Lt (horse-drawn) Infantry
    Supply Columns
10/1. Lt (mot.) Fuel Column
1. Supply Coy
1. (mot.) Maint Coy

1. (mot.) Bakery Coy
1. (mot.) Butcher Coy
1. Divisional Admin
1/1. Medical Coy
2/1. (mot.) Medical Coy
1. Ambulance Coy
1. Veterinary Troop
1. (mot.) MP Detachment
1. (mot.) Field Post Office

The light column (*leichte Kolonne*), found in most types of infantry regiments, consisted of 39 wagons carrying all types of supplies except rations. It served as a supply reserve for the subordinate battalions. The administrative troops included civilian specialists (*Beamte*) in various positions. The rations supply office (*Verpflegungsamt*) handled the requisitioning and supply of rations for troop units. Both butcher and bakery companies tried to procure as much locally possible. The supply organization stepped in once stores reached the railheads. Army columns took the supplies from the railheads to the army dumps, from where the divisional supply companies moved them from the divisional collecting points. There the battalion columns picked them up and delivered them to the combat troops through battalion or company distribution points; troops themselves could go to the points for resupply. It was a flexible system that allowed for the creation of ad hoc *Kampfgruppen*.

The company supplies were handled by *Troße* (trains): *Gefechtstroß* (battle train, which included armorers, a blacksmith and wheelwright), *Verpflegungstroß* (rations train) and

Most German supplies—here a mobile kitchen—were horse-drawn wagons—particularly when muddy seasons meant most vehicles couldn't move. *NARA*

Gepäcktroß (baggage train, including tailer, cobbler, and clerk), although the Volksgrenadier-Division lost the *Troße* and centralized equipment, rations, and cooking duties in battalion supply platoons. From 1942–43 onward Hiwis were included on strength and were often employed as wagon drivers—the Type 1944 Division had 98 allocated, the VGD had 40.

Feldpost—Field Post

Soldiers were encouraged to write home and whilst they were not allowed to give details of operations, there was little censorship compared with the Allies. Every army has some form of field post office to enable troops to send and receive mail. It's important for morale. Indeed, historically there are letters extant from ancient Roman soldiers in Africa asking for people from home to send them things and it was no different on the Eastern Front. To maintain security, *Feldpostbriefe* (field post letters) were not addressed by unit but with a five-digit number—each Wehrmacht unit had a different one, which changed on occasion—and as a unit moved around each new area it was allocated a unique postal code. Letters and packets were transported towards the front in field post trains to a field post control center from where the FPOs of the divisions or army troops took over, sorting according to the field post numbers assigned to them.

Mail handling in the Russian winter—from railhead to *Panjewagon*. NARA

Aerial Resupply

One of the methods used to resupply German troops in the Soviet Union, aerial resupply proved to be less than successful and tended to be used mainly as a last resort. To begin with, an air force needs a lot of materiel to be able to resupply a unit of any size: as well as sufficient transport aircraft there need to be suitable personnel and airfields to load and unload the cargo; the important infrastructure—air traffic control, refuelling and ground crew; fighters to fly protection—and, of course, the weather to be able to fly missions and see where the supplies needed to be delivered.

The biggest problem the Luftwaffe had was lack of suitable aircraft. The venerable "*Tante-Ju*," the Junkers Ju 52/3m, was its workhorse but it was too small (payload around 4,000kg) and too slow (top speed of 265kph) to carry significant cargo unless used in high numbers—and after the battles in the West and over Crete, there were never enough. The Netherlands campaign saw 167 lost and Crete 270. The Luftwaffe had 552 Ju 52s at the start of the war but between 1939 and 1944, it only received 2,804 more (145 in 1939, 338 in 1940, 502 in 1941, 503 in 1942, 887 in 1943, and 379 in 1944). Production ended in summer 1944.

At Demyansk, the resupply was sufficient to allow the pocket to be sustained. Between early February and the relief of the pocket in May, Demyansk and Cholm were delivered 59,000 tons of supplies and 31,000 replacement troops, much by over 100 flights a day by Ju 52s. Over 36,000 wounded were also evacuated. The problem was the cost: 265 aircraft including 106 Ju 52s.

The success at Demyansk convinced both Göring and Hitler that Stalingrad could be supplied from the air. The trouble was that they hadn't done their math.

Supplying 6. Armee in Stalingrad proved too much for the Luftwaffe. It simply didn't have the number of transport aircraft required. *SF collection*

6. Armee needed 500–750 tons of supplies a day. Luftwaffe staff reckoned they'd need over 10,000 Ju 52s to handle that. The whole Luftwaffe at the time only had 750. In reality, the Luftwaffe managed 8,250 tons all told, an average of 114.6 tons a day. The weather, loss of airfields to the Soviets, and no construction of additional airfields tipped the balance in favor of the Soviets. Generaloberst Friedrich Paulus, noted:

> When the aircraft do not land, it means the death of the army. Now it is in any case already too late. Every machine that lands saves the lives of 1,000 men. ... Dropping the supplies does no good. Many supply canisters are not found, as we have no fuel with which to retrieve them. Today is the fourth day my people have had nothing to eat. We could not recover our heavy weapons, because we have no fuel. They are lost. Our last horses have been eaten. Can you picture the soldiers diving on an old horse cadaver, breaking open its head, and devouring its brains raw?

The Germans also tried using gliders to resupply the fortresses. Resupply for the Budapest garrison was often carried by glider but the loss of the main airfield on January 9, 1945, forced the garrison to use the Vérmezo meadow near the Royal Castle in Buda. The last mission took place on February 5, 1945. Six DFS 230s landed carrying 97 tonnes of ammunition, 10 tonnes of fuel, 28 tonnes of food, and four engine-oil drums and spare parts crates. After the loss of the airfield 36 DFS 230s transported ammunition, fuel, food, medical supplies, and flour. The losses in the Budapest operation had been severe: 48 gliders had landed but at a cost of 36 Ju 52s and nine other aircraft. During the breakout, the fleeing troops were airdropped supplies on February 14 (by nine He 111s) and on the 15th (by nine He 111s and three Ju 52s).

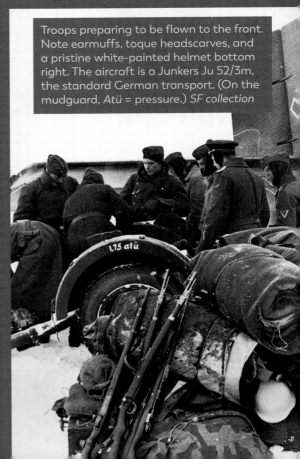

Troops preparing to be flown to the front. Note earmuffs, toque headscarves, and a pristine white-painted helmet bottom right. The aircraft is a Junkers Ju 52/3m, the standard German transport. (On the mudguard, *Atü* = pressure.) *SF collection*

In the last months of the war various small units of Luftflotte 6 (under Generaloberst Otto Deßloch) flew from Hohenmauth and Königgrätz and from Stolp-Reitz to Elbing; Finow and Stettin-Altdamm to Arnswalde; and Alt-Lönnewitz to Posen, Glogau, and Breslau. From Sagan-Küpper, resupply missions were flown to Gruppe Nehring (General Walther Nehring's XXIV. Panzerkorps) and Gruppe von Saucken (General Dietrich von Saucken of Panzerkorps Großdeutschland) as they and their "*Wandernden Kessel*" (moving pocket) negotiated their way back to German lines on January 19–31. The last glider resupply to Breslau and Berlin flew on April 30.

Medical Services

There are many facets to military medical services, but they start with treating wounded soldiers, often a difficulty in a mobile war:

> To evacuate wounded soldiers early on in Mogilev was impossible. We had more than 1,000 wounded soldiers in the town, and it was ordered by division that those should be handed over to the Russians. The division surgeon had this order, and he took a Red Cross flag and went to the Russians, but they shot him down, and I know from my later time in Russian captivity that most of the wounded in my division had no chance because they had no help. Later we took every wounded man with us if possible, and nobody wanted to be released. In some cases, we had the possibility of using ambulances which we found. At Minsk we thought we were in the German lines, but actually we were again surrounded. Thereafter, only the lighter wounded stayed with the combat group.

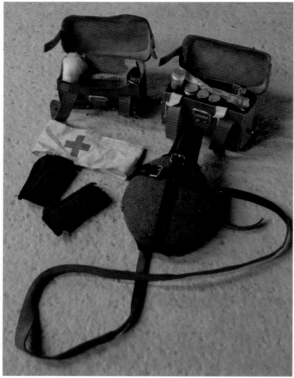

Our reenactor wears a red cross armband and carries an extra, larger water bottle as well as two medical pouches. There were a few types of stamped pouch: T for *Träger* (stretcher-bearers) and S for *Sanitäter* (medic) for example. These contained bandages, tourniquets, field dressings, tweezers, scissors, pins, and so on. The larger water bottle has a Bakelite cup for medicine. The use of the red cross armband wasn't universal as it was seen as being a target for Soviet snipers. *SF*

Stretchers were essential for moving casualties. This one has two large canvas straps to stop the casualty falling off. The difference between *Krankenträger* (stretcher bearer) and *Hilfskrankenträger* (auxiliary stretcher bearer) is that the former belonged to the *Sanitätsdienst* (medical service) and were specifically trained for their mission. This included training as medical orderlies during which they their did duty in medical installations. The regular soldiers appointed as *Hilfskrankenträger* had only rudimentary first aid training and remained with their units. *SF collection*

Wounds were not always the result of enemy action. Many soldiers contracted some form of illness or suffered from non-combat wounds such as frostbite. In the Ostheer's first dreadful winter of 1941–42, according to statistics compiled later by OKW, the number of frostbite cases totaled 141,957 by March 31, 1942. Of these, 1,424 required amputations. However, the figures are difficult to pin down. Liedtke identifies:

> Between December 1, 1941, and May 1, 1942, combat casualties in the East amounted to an approximate 418,322. In contrast, during this timeframe some 414,028 men were listed as sick or frostbitten, but this only includes those whose treatment required their transfer back to Germany. The actual number of the sick and frostbitten was probably much greater.

Each German soldier carried two first aid packets, one large and one small. Additionally, inside the tunic there was a small, thin interior pocket that was designed to hold a *Verbandpäckchen* (bandage). Other items that were often carried in tunic pockets included extra bandages and salves to treat such things as frostbite and cold weather sores. Another common item was foot powder, which also came in a small tin container. Most vehicles carried a first aid kit in a tin box containing bandages, tourniquets, splints, iodine and other ointments, various tablets and antiseptics, equipment—scissors, tweezers, safety pins—and a first aid guide.

At the lowest unit level—the one closest to the front line—the first line of medics were the *Krankenträger* (stretcher-bearers). They had up to eight weeks' training in first aid and moving the wounded who couldn't walk. Some *Krankenträger* had other jobs such as motorcycle dispatch riders. The stretchers came in two equal-sized, collapsible halves, easily carried and assembled. If conditions permitted, they could be transported on two-wheeled carriers. In addition to the *Krankenträger*, several men in each unit—around eight—were appointed as *Hilfskrankenträger* (auxiliary stretcher-bearers). They were either regular soldiers or, later in the war, Hiwis. As in many other armies, bandsmen were often used as *Hilfskrankenträger*.

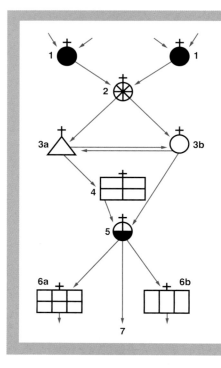

Evacuation

1. Wounded arrive at the *Verwundetennest* (battalion aid post).
2. If they cannot walk, they are picked by ambulance at a *Wagenhalteplatz* (ambulance post).
3. From there they are taken to the *Hauptverbandplatz* (field dressing station) or *Leichtverwundetensammelplatz* (collecting point for lightly wounded).
4. The badly wounded are taken to the *Feldlazarett* (divisional field hospital).
5. The badly wounded and lightly wounded are taken/make their way to the *Krankensammelstelle* (casualty collection point).
6. They end up in either a *Kriegslazarett* (army field hospital) or a *Leichtkrankenkriegslazarett* (army field hospital for the lightly wounded).
7. Those who need further treatment are sent to hospitals/to recuperate in Germany while the lightly wounded return via an *Ersatz* (replacement) unit to the front.

The stretcher-bearers would take the wounded to the *Verwundetennest* (platoon/company aid station). Here they would be helped by the *Sanitätsunteroffizier* (a trained medical NCO or, sometimes, a private assigned to each unit). There was usually a single "*Sani*" in each company. He would have had six months' training at a *Sanitätsstaffel* and may have gone on additional courses. He would usually wear a red cross armband and a medical branch symbol on his forearm; all the medical personnel, including the stretcher-bearers, were supposed to wear red cross armbands but some didn't as it was felt that they acted as targets for Soviet snipers. They carried two medical pouches on their belt and were armed with a pistol or rifle. The

One of Kurt Kranz's sketches from *Winteralltag im Urwald Lapplands* (*Everyday winter life in the primeval forests of Lapland*, the northern part of Finland). A ski patrol uses an *akja* (boat sledge) to pull a casualty through the snow. The rear man controls the descent. In deep snow the Germans made excellent use of the *akja* as a supplementary piece of equipment. RCT

Verwundetennest was in an extreme forward position but, where possible, this was where a wounded man probably received the first dressing, splinting, or tourniquet.

The next point of call for the wounded was the battalion aid post (*Truppenverbandplatz*) where the *Bataillonsarzt* (battalion MO) and his assistant (*Assistenzarzt* or *Hilfsarzt*) practiced. From battalion the wounded travelled either by ambulance (having been picked up at the ambulance car post—*Wagenhalteplatz*) to a *Hauptverbandplatz* (field clearing station set up by the division) or the walking wounded went to a *Leichtverwundetensammelplatz* (collection point for lightly wounded). Motor ambulances could take either four lying, or two lying and four sitting, or eight sitting patients.

Divisional medical facilities—under the command of a *Divisionsarzt* (divional MO, IVb of the divisional staff)—usually comprised two medical companies, a motorized field hospital (with accommodation for 200 patients), and two motor ambulance trains (each having 15 ambulances, sometimes with one motorized and one horse-drawn. Some mobile units had a third motorized ambulance train rather than a hospital).

At the beginning of the war in Europe, all divisions had two *Sanitäts Kompanien* (medical companies), one mechanized and the other horse-drawn, although in some divisions both were mechanized. In action, one platoon established a field dressing station and a lightly wounded collecting post; it included at least one surgeon-specialist. The second was the stretcher-bearer platoon; the third was held in reserve. Usually, an ambulance car post was also formed. Medical companies set up the division aid station from canvas when they couldn't find anything suitable. The benefit of having a motorized company was that it could keep up which the fluid advances that started the campaign.

From the *Hauptverbandplatz* seriously wounded men were evacuated to the *Feldlazarett* or to a *Kriegslazarett* (divisional or army field hospital).

To keep the medical services with combat units properly supplied at all times a medical supply depot was allocated to each Armee. This depot was able to establish branch depots where and when it deemed such stations necessary.

Nicknamed "*Sankas*" or "*Sankras*" (from *Sanitätskraftwagen*), Kfz31 *Krankenkraftwagen* (German motor ambulances such as the Opel Blitz Typ S, Phänomen-Granit 25H, Steyr 640 or smaller Phänomen-Granit 1500A, and Mercedes-Benz LE1100) were usually configured to take either four lying, or two lying and four sitting, or eight sitting patients. Some buses could also be fitted with stretcher racks to carry wounded. Air evacuation was less frequent. *WikiCommons/Sangreal reworked by TJ.MD (CC BY-SA 3.0)*

Strategy and Tactics

Adolf Hitler made himself more and more involved in dictating the German Army's strategy and tactics. His intervention led to a confrontation between the long-held command philosophy of the Prussian and German armies— *Auftragstaktik*—and his insistence on an inflexible adherence to his diktats. The Germans were used to giving broad, mission-orientated directives which allowed junior officers to use discretion and imagination in fulfilling tasks. Hitler, however, expected unconditional obedience to the letter of his orders—allowing no flexibility. This meant that an army used to mobile defense was forced into the straitjacket of holding firm. It also led senior officers to overcontrol their subordinates—and the subordinates to become afraid to act without express permission from above.

The subservience of those surrounding Hitler added to the problem. The image of Hitler moving paper units that had no bearing on reality around his command map with his Oberkommando staff afraid to step in has a strong whiff of truth. While his orders were proving intuitive and successful in the 1930s, it was easy not to doubt, but by 1944 the views of many on the ground had changed.

As an example, Major Heinz-Georg Lemm was convinced that the Russian offensive that we now know as Operation *Bagration* was heading straight for him near Mogilev in today's Belarus. For weeks there had been obvious signs: reconnaissance aircraft, artillery registering their guns from new positions, preparation of tank lanes in wooded areas on the other side of the river from his positions, and heavy traffic in the enemy's hinterland. "During my time in Russia rarely did all signs point so clearly to an imminent major attack," Lemm said when he reported the information. In mid-June the corps commander, General der Artillerie Robert Martinek, visited the position and satisfied himself that the reports were correct. However, he told Lemm that at the Wolfsschanze, the Führer's HQ in Prussia, the offensive was expected in the south and what Lemm could see was

Presumed Soviet operational intentions and current enemy deployment of forces as of AM June 13, 1944. Lemm was convinced that the attack was going to come where he was in Byelorussia, but the OKW thought otherwise—thanks to intelligence reports that suggested attacks farther south. *SF collection*

only Soviet *maskirovka*—deception and diversionary measures. "When leaving he [Martinek] gloomily said, 'Whom the gods would destroy, they first make mad.' It was clear that he meant nobody else but Hitler, the Supreme Commander of the German Armed Forces."

The Infantry Squad

The keystone of infantry tactics, the infantry squad, changed in composition during the war. The 1939 infantry battalion rifle platoon had three 13-man squads: an NCO in charge and an NCO 2IC, a four-man LMG troop, plus a rifle troop of seven men. This changed in 1940 when an extra squad was added to the rifle platoon and the squad size was reduced to 10 men (as shown below). It was made up of a squad leader and nine others, and the squad was set up around the machine gun it carried (usually an MG 34 or, latterly, an MG 42; some would have even had the older MG 08 or 15).The 1943 *neue Art* (*nA*) division had a further reduction in squad size to nine men—the leader and one other with machine pistols, the LMG gunner with a pistol, and the other six men with rifles, one with a grenade launcher. Losses in the east meant that many

Patrolling was essential for battlefield reconnaissance, for intelligence—to take prisoners—or to raid or ambush the enemy. *NAC*

squads had seen a force reduction in size before this change. Around 1942–43 the MG 42 and Gewehr 43 started to appear, although many German infantrymen made use of captured Soviet weapons, particularly the PPSh41 SMG. The 1944 Volksgrenadier company had three platoons—two Sturm (equipped where possible with StG 44 assault rifles) and one rifle. The former had two squads of nine men (including an NCO IC) all armed with assault rifles, and a third squad with an LMG and four men armed with Kar98k rifles. The rifle platoon had three squads of nine men (NCO and 2IC with machine pistols, an LMG, and six riflemen). This changed in 1944 when the squad size was cut to eight in the Sturm platoons, two of the squads armed with StG 44s, the other squad composed of leader/two LMG two-man teams/three riflemen. The rifle platoon squads were also cut to eight men. Interestingly, the VGD ORBAT included six sharpshooters in Company HQ and the rifle grenades moved to Platoon HQ.

The German squad throughout the war was based on the LMG. In firefights it was able to provide the heaviest concentration of fire against the most threatening and dangerous targets. The assistant gunner helps ready the gun for action and then lies down to the left rear and remains ready to assist the machine-gunner with stoppages and barrel changing or by replacing him if he is hit. *SF collection*

Squad Organization and Equipment

Squad leader commands his squad. He directs the fire of the light machine gun and, in so far as the combat permits, that of the riflemen also. He is responsible for the mechanical condition of the weapons and equipment, and for the availability of ammunition within his squad. He carries a machine pistol with six magazines (each with 32 rounds) in magazine pouches, magazine loader, field glasses, wire cutters, pocket compass, signal whistle, sunglasses, and spotlight.

Machine-gunner (No. 1) The machine-gunner operates the machine gun in battle. He is responsible for the care of the weapon. He carries an MG 34 or MG 42 with belt, magazine 34 (50 rounds), tool pouch, pistol, short spade, sunglasses, and spotlight.

MG assistant (No. 2) This member of the squad is the assistant to the machine-gunner in combat. He insures the supply of ammunition. He assists the machine-gunner in the preparation for firing and in going into position. Then he usually takes position under cover, several paces to the left flank or rear of the machine-gunner. He is always ready to aid the machine-gunner (for example, by correcting jams, changing barrels, righting the gun on bipod) or to replace him. After the gun has gone into position, if there is suitable cover present, he lies down near the machine-gunner and aids him in serving the machine gun. He also aids the machine-gunner in the care of the weapon. He carries a barrel protector (with a spare barrel), four belt drums (each 50 rounds), ammunition belt, pistol, ammunition box (300 rounds), short spade, and sunglasses.

Ammunition-carrier (No. 3) If possible, the ammunition-carrier takes a position to the rear, under cover. He inspects the ammunition belts and ammunition. He also operates as a close-in or hand-to-hand fighter. He carries a barrel protector (with a spare barrel), two ammunition boxes (each with 300 rounds), ammunition belt, rifle, and short spade.

Riflemen (Nos. 4–9) The riflemen execute close-combat fighting with rifle fire and bayonet. One rifleman is the second-in-command. He is the assistant to the squad leader and commands the squad in the absence of the leader. He is responsible for liaison with the platoon commander and with adjacent squads. He carries a rifle, two ammunition pouches, and a short spade. When ordered he also carries hand grenades, smoke grenades, explosive charges, ammunition, and a machine-gun tripod.

Patrol activities are chiefly the tasks of rifle companies and an important link in their training (as is intensive observation of the battlefield) patrols must have fighting power.

The MG 34 was capable of a rate of fire of 1,000 rounds per minute, although more common was 200–500 with controlled fire. The gunner carried a toolbox on his belt. It contained cleaning rods and a pull-through with assorted brushes and cloth, oil, various small tools, a spare bolt, and an AA ring sight. *SF collection*

Breakout from the Cherkassy Pocket

Tthe German line along Dnieper crumbled to a strong attack and by February 6, 1944, what remained of XLII. and XI. Armeekorps was encircled. They became Gruppe Stemmermann (the commander of XI. Korps). The gradual shrinking of the pocket had the benefit of concentrating the forces—an important prerequisite for the eventual breakout. This attempt also needed a relief thrust from the outside, mainly by III. Panzerkorps. The start of the muddy season postponed the breakout and complicated matters for both attackers and defenders. On February 14 elements of XLII. Korps took Khilki and Komarovka to provide a good jump-off line. Three divisional columns advanced: Korps detachment B (from 8. Armee), 5. SS-Panzer-Division Wiking, and 72. Infanterie-Division. The divisions were organized in five waves: 1. An infantry regiment reinforced by a battery of light artillery (at least eight horses per gun, plus spares) and one engineer company. 2. Antitank and assault gun units. 3. Remainder of infantry (minus one battalion), engineers, and light artillery. 4. Those wounded fit to be transported, accompanied by an infantry battalion. 5. Supply and service units. The rearguard, under Stemmermann, who died in action, was composed of 57. and 88. Infanterie-Divisionen. The breakout ended with at least 40,000 Germans killed, wounded, or captured (including those outside the pocket). Soviet losses were around 80,000. The Germans saved many of their men but lost most of their heavy equipment—and 32 vital transport aircraft during resupply operations.

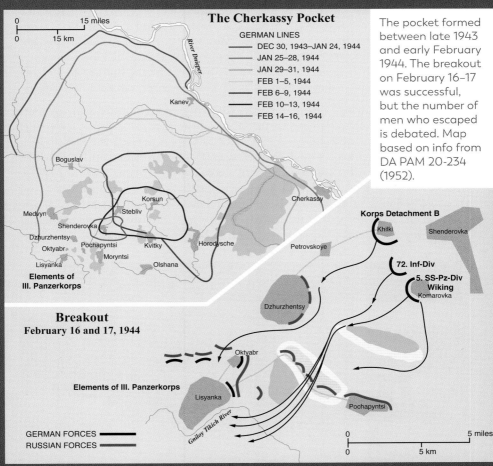

The Cherkassy Pocket

GERMAN LINES

— DEC 30, 1943–JAN 24, 1944
— JAN 25–28, 1944
— JAN 29–31, 1944
— FEB 1–5, 1944
— FEB 6–9, 1944
— FEB 10–13, 1944
— FEB 14–16, 1944

0   15 miles
0   15 km

River Dnieper

Kanev

Boguslav

Korsun

Stebliv

Cherkassy

Medvyn

Shenderovka

Dzhurzhentsy

Oktyabr   Pochapyntsi   Kvitky   Horodysche

Moryntsi

Lisyanka   Olshana

Elements of III. Panzerkorps

The pocket formed between late 1943 and early February 1944. The breakout on February 16–17 was successful, but the number of men who escaped is debated. Map based on info from DA PAM 20-234 (1952).

Korps Detachment B

Khilki

Shenderovka

72. Inf-Div

5. SS-Pz-Div Wiking

Komarovka

Petrovskoye

Dzhurzhentsy

**Breakout
February 16 and 17, 1944**

Oktyabr

Elements of III. Panzerkorps

Lisyanka

Pochapyntsi

Gniloy Tikich River

GERMAN FORCES ▬▬▬
RUSSIAN FORCES ▬▬▬

0   5 miles
0   5 km

MG team loading up to cross the Dnieper. This was a significant operation that saw a river assault crossing on August 31 in the Kremenchug area. German accounts mention hundreds of assault boats mainly of two types—capable of carrying 4 to 6 or 10 to 16 men. Both were driven by outboard motors. (An Eigener sketch.) *RCT*

River Crossing and Bridging

When the Germans reached a river, the first stage would be an assault crossing by infantry in storm boats. They were followed by men in other pneumatic boats. Once a bridgehead had been established, troops were flooded across by ferrying, rafts or light bridges if the river wasn't too wide. More substantial bridges—or bridge repair—followed.

The Germans did test tracked bridgelayers using the PzKpfw IV chassis—the Brückenleger IV. In all 20 were produced with a 9m bridge that had a 28-ton capacity. Too heavy for its suspension, the tank was canceled. Most were converted back to regular gun tanks. In January 1941, Krupp built four of an improved Brückenleger IVc that saw service in 1941 in Russia with 3. Panzer-Division. Built in parallel with the Brückenleger IV, the Infanterie-Sturmstegpanzer allowed foot soldiers to cross obstacles with extensible ladders.

The German Army had a range of bridges (*Brückengeräte*) and the bridging columns (*Brückenkolonnen*—shortened to *Brücko*) that erected them. The basic transport tools of the Brückenkolonnen were the *Bockwagen* (Pf 8, 10 or 14 support wagons), the *Pontonwagen* (Pf 9, 11 or 15 pontoon wagons) and *Rampenwagen* (Pf 12 ramp wagons) that carried the bridge parts. For example, a Brückegerät B had a nominal TOE (1 June 1944) of 1 officer, 20 NCOs, 104 men, 41 vehicles (lorries, motorcycles, SdKfz 7s, and a Schwimmwagen) and was carried by 8 Pf 8s, 16 Pf 9s, 2 Pf 12s, and had 2 trailers for assault dinghies (*Anhänger für Sturmboote*) and 2 for motorboats (*Anhänger für M-Boote*). The majority of the bridging equipment was lorry- or halftrack-drawn but a lot of it could be horse-drawn.

Many rivers could simply be forded. This is an SdKfz 11 with a 7.5cm *leichte Feldkanone* 38. The rope is a guideline. *NARA*

Extended *Flossacke* 34 assault pontoon bridge. The engineer battalion usually had a bridging column, but these were sometimes grouped together and assigned from the army GHQ engineer pool, particularly if the division was operating in terrain where bridging was unnecessary. In 1942 this ad hoc arrangement was confirmed, and the bridging columns became independent. There were several different bridge types, perhaps the most important in the early war years being the Type B medium combat bridge. These others included light recce bridges (Type D), light combat bridges (Type C), mountain bridges (Type G), and the medium combat Type T bridges, of Czech design, which were attached to many infantry divisions in both motorized and horse-drawn forms. *SF collection*

Fixed Strongpoints and Fortresses

Hitler's Führer Order No. 11 of March 8, 1944 (Commanders of the Fixed Strongpoints and Combat Commanders) identified 29 towns that were to become *Festen Plätzen* (fixed strongpoints):

> The "fixed strongpoints" are to serve the same purpose as formerly the fortresses. They are to prevent the enemy from seizing these operationally important spots. They must permit themselves to be surrounded, thereby tying up as strong enemy forces as possible. Thereby they will create favorable circumstances for successful counteroperations. … Only the Commanding General of the Army Group in person with my permission can relieve the commander of the fixed strongpoint of his task, and possibly order that the fixed strongpoint be abandoned.

Commanding officer of I./Fusilier Regiment 27 was Major Heinz-Georg Lemm who remembered:

> The politicians believed the Führer order would motivate the troops. In reality, every unit tried to avoid any place that possibly could become a Festen Platz, either to bypass those towns and not approach them or to try to defend long before a town and then shift, in one leap, to go around the town to avoid being found in a Festen Platz.

In the case of Mogilev, one of the strongpoints identified by the Führer Order, Generalleutnant Rudolf Bamler was in command. In the last days of the defense, he was a nervous wreck. Lemm continued:

> General Bamler … could say no more than "I have taken an oath and I have to be here." The 1A and I asked General Bamler to give the order for breakout but he asked to discuss the situation with the division judge [legal officer]. The general asked the judge, "What will happen if I give the order to break out?" The judge was a very logical man and he answered, "In that case you will be courtmartialed for disobedience." General Bamler replied, "Now you have seen what will happen if I give the order." The 1A stated, "I think it is better for a general to end up in front of an execution squad than the 8,000 men in this town." General Bamler left the room.

Lemm's battalion was tasked with keeping the last bridge to Mogilev open until the remaining combat teams of 31st and 337th Divisions got across. Then he received an order from the division in Mogilev: "Break off battle immediately. Battalion to hold itself at Division's disposal, Urgent." The entire battalion, including wounded, mounted trucks and moved back towards the Dnieper bridge, covered by the last three assault guns. As soon as the last vehicle of the convoy crossed, the engineers fired demolition charges. "Why are you in such a hurry?" Lemm asked the engineer officer, who handed over his binoculars and pointed across the river. There, 1,000 meters away, Lemm saw a column of at least 60 T-34s moving quickly towards the bridge. Only five minutes later and the battalion wouldn't have reached the western bank. Lemm asked Bamler for orders. "The general," Lemm remembered, "shrugs his shoulders and only says: 'There is nothing you can do here anymore. I have no sensible mission for you.'"

Lemm made a quick decision and decided to leave the town. As it got dark his battalion broke out. Overrunning Russian infantry and knocking out three enemy tanks, the battalion made its way to the north. Eventually, he met his regimental commander who told him that three hours after the breakout Mogilev was seized by the Russians. Bamler and over 3,000 men ended up being taken into captivity. (Bamler ended up in East Germany working for the Stasi.)

When Heinz Guderian became acting chief of the OKH in July 1944, he started a building program to turn several cities in Germany and Poland into fortresses. With the Luftwaffe providing aerial resupply as far as it was possible, these fortresses proved to be difficult to take and many didn't fall until April, their garrisons bolstered by retreating troops. Breslau and Olmütz held out until two days before the final surrender.

Was it a sensible strategy? Hitler bottled up 200,000 men in Courland: they and the defenders of the fortresses could, perhaps, have been put to better use. Certainly, Guderian believed this. All the fortresses eventually fell to the Red Army—but it took special efforts to take them and enabled citizen soldiers such as the Volkssturm to participate directly in the battles in a way they couldn't have done in open warfare. The Soviets paused in their surge toward Berlin and stopped to sort out the "Baltic Balcony" and the fortresses there. The strategy also reinforced the nihilism of the Nazi regime in its final death throes. It enabled commanders to force citizens to fight to the bitter end and murder hundreds labeled cowards or backsliders; it also led to the complete destruction of some of Germany's most historic cities.

Improvisation

The German Army was faced with a great calamity as early as the muddy period and winter of 1941–42. Top-level staffs and field forces alike were forced to improvise extensively. As the campaign wore on and the German military potential continued to decline, improvisations of the widest variety became increasingly prevalent. Toward the end of the war the ratio of strength between the German and Soviet armies became so disproportionate that improvisations, especially in combat operations, were rampant. Finally, the entire conduct of war was one great improvisation. These are some examples:

Tank Riding

In pursuit, German and enemy infantry found it helpful to mount on tanks—for example, when 6. Panzer-Division spearheaded Heeresgruppe Nord in July 1941 the Russians were dislodged and dispersed. The division had to hurry forward to take three major bridges before they could be demolished and allow the enemy to set up a defensive position. Spearhead units—each some 50 tanks strong—with mounted infantry pursued the Russians relentlessly, occupied the bridges, and reached the day's objective, the city of Ostrov, within three hours.

Another example was during a battle fought southeast of Plavskoye in Heeresgruppe Mitte's sector in November 1941. After a Soviet cavalry division attacked an exposed flank *Sturmgeschütze* were sent with infantry hanging on "like grapes on a vine. They rode into the enemy lines with all guns ablaze. The enemy cavalry division was obliterated."

Column of StuG III Ausf Gs in Slovakia led by a command version (note the star antenna). The commander on the front has a *Wolchowstock* walking stick. Named after the River Wolchow (German spelling of Volkhov) in the Leningrad area, these sticks were carved by the men for their commanders. Sometimes produced by the wounded, occasionally by Soviet POWs, they were treasured items. He is wearing the double-breasted field gray uniform worn by Panzerjäger and Sturmgeschütz units. *NAC*

Even construction companies were used as infantry when needs must. *SF collection*

But if the enemy was firmly entrenched, tank riding could be very dangerous, particularly in the face of antitank weapons and air attacks. The Russians used this method all the time but suffered heavy casualties from machine-gun fire.

Combat Engineers as Infantry

The Germans were often forced to employ combat engineer units as infantry, wasting irreplaceable specialists even though commanders understood the difficulties they were laying up for themselves. The trouble was that when things were critical, needs must—and combat engineers had received infantry training. On many occasions the courage and steadfastness of the engineers saved the day. For example, when the enemy broke through southwest of Rzhev in 1942, "a corps engineer regiment, all engineer units of one division, and even all the construction engineer companies and some of the road-building battalions from the vicinity were committed to stop the Russian thrust into the rear of 9. Armee"—which they did but at some cost. During the last year of the war, when it was all hands to the pumps and manpower problems were growing more and more acute, many field commanders were compelled to sacrifice their specialized troops.

Tactical Retreats

Zone defense tactics, which were introduced toward the end of the war, were derived from an analysis of the reasons for the success of most enemy breakthroughs. The principal factors to be considered were the following:

- The annihilation of front-line troops by mass concentration on points along the main line of resistance;
- The neutralization or destruction of the artillery by heavy counterbattery fire and continuous air attacks;
- The elimination of command staffs by air attacks and surprise fire on command posts up to army level;
- The harassing of reserves by artillery fire and air attacks on their assembly areas;
- The disruption of the routes of communication to the front which delayed movements of reserves and cut off supply;
- The massed armored thrusts in depth which enabled the Russians to obtain freedom of maneuver.

The task of the defender was to find some way to neutralize or reduce the effectiveness of these tactics. The Germans came up with two ways: either by constructing bombproof and shellproof positions or by withdrawing the forward units in time to evade the devastating barrages. Doing the former was difficult with fluid fronts—easy in Normandy but not so easy in the vastness of the Soviet Union. The latter hinged on making the decision to move from the battle positions to safety at the right time, and returning in time to face the enemy attack.

German Defensive Doctrine

Though German defensive methods were a kaleidoscope of improvisation, certain basic principles remained constant and formed the true heart of German doctrine. The German Army's defensive methods were derived from four basic principles: depth, maneuver, firepower, and counterattack. Through all the variations in defensive methods, these principles continued to guide German commanders in conducting their operations.

After World War I the Germans made radical changes to their offensive doctrine, taking on board the changes brought about by the arrival of the tank and the developments to airpower. This led to Blitzkrieg. However, unlike their offense, the German defensive doctrine was much more conservative. In 1941 it was based on positional warfare (*Stellungskrieg*) and elastic defense. It was more important to defeat the enemy with the minimum loss to defending forces rather than clinging onto terrain for the sake of prestige. *Truppenführung*, which was published in 1933 and replaced *Führung und Gefecht der verbundenen Waffen* (Leadership and Combat of Combined Arms) as the basic German operations manual, promoted elastic defense in depth. Indeed, the 1933 version of the elastic defense consisted of the same three defensive zones as had appeared in Ludendorff's original concept, but with an additional advanced position posted in front.

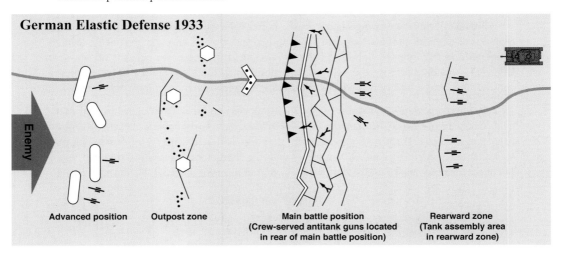

German Elastic Defense 1933

Enemy

| Advanced position | Outpost zone | Main battle position (Crew-served antitank guns located in rear of main battle position) | Rearward zone (Tank assembly area in rearward zone) |

The doctrine would be severely tested during the winter battles of 1941 because it was predicated on any sustained defensive fighting being borne by infantry divisions, supported only as necessary by panzers held in reserve for counterattack—and that there would be sufficient infantrymen to organize a cohesive defense in depth.

Defensive Practice in Winter 1941

At the tactical level, German defensive practice during the winter of 1941 was dictated by Hitler's stand-fast order, the appalling weakness of German units, and the harshness of the Russian winter weather. These three factors forced the Germans to use a defensive system that consisted mostly of a network of loosely connected strongpoints backed by local reserves.

The weakness was significant. After six months of the fighting, Soviet attacks had reduced the average rifle company strength from 10 NCOs and 60 men on December 7 to five NCOs and 20 men just five days later. Panzergruppe 3 on December 19 reported its XLI. and LVI. Panzerkorps fielded only 1,821 and 900 total combatants respectively. To generate greater infantry strength, men from nonessential rear services were hurried forward, as were troops from artillery and antitank batteries whose weapons had been destroyed or abandoned.

But on top of the battle casualties the subzero temperatures and the paucity of suitable clothing and equipment added to the German woes: even when the Soviet winter counteroffensive developed, cold-weather casualties exceeded combat losses in most German units. One infantry regiment, heavily engaged at the beginning of the Soviet attack, estimated that its losses in two days of fighting amounted to only 100 battle casualties compared to 800 cases of frostbite.

To find shelter from the weather, the German soldiers moved into the towns and villages. It was important to choose buildings that were defendable or could be made so, by banking snow against the outer, reinforcing overhead and cutting firing embrasures. If possible, 2cm flak guns were integrated into the defense to produce "flak nests" that worked against aircraft and infantry. There were drawbacks: it was easy to spot the defended houses and attack them, and the strongpoint approach left control of the area to the Red Army, especially at night.

Because of this the Germans had to push out from the villages to improve their security, despite the renewed problems of cold. They did so by creating an outer perimeter, a line of interconnected infantry fighting positions, circling this central strongpoint (as shown below). Eventually these were developed to include small bunkers that could be warmed, communications paths, improved fields of fire, and the emplacement of mines and obstacles.

The bunkers were separated from the fighting positions (see sketch opposite, top) and held about six men. The *Taschenbuch für den Winterkrieg* (*Pocketbook for Winter Warfare* dated August 5, 1942) provided suggestions for the construction of winter positions using logs, packed snow, *Sandeis* (ice concrete), sandbags, blasting charges for dugouts and trenches, and, of course, heating facilities, including stoves and how to make charcoal. Defenses included

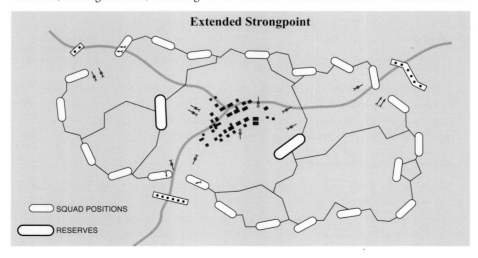

Extended Strongpoint

SQUAD POSITIONS

RESERVES

antitank obstacles made from packed snow, antitank traps in frozen bodies of water, barbed-wire rolls, and mines—although these were a problem in snow and tripwires were seen as being more effective.

The trouble with this approach was that the Soviets were adept at infiltration and spreading strongpoints too far apart ran the risk—even with patrols—of being surrounded. The only answer was to reduce the size of the gaps and defend in depth, placing artillery and antitank guns in depth to allow them to fire on any Soviet infiltration.

As the Soviet winter offensive petered out, Hitler congratulated himself and told anyone who'd listen that it was his tactical awareness that had "saved" the Ostheer and that the tactic of standing fast was here to stay. It would prove to be a fatal error.

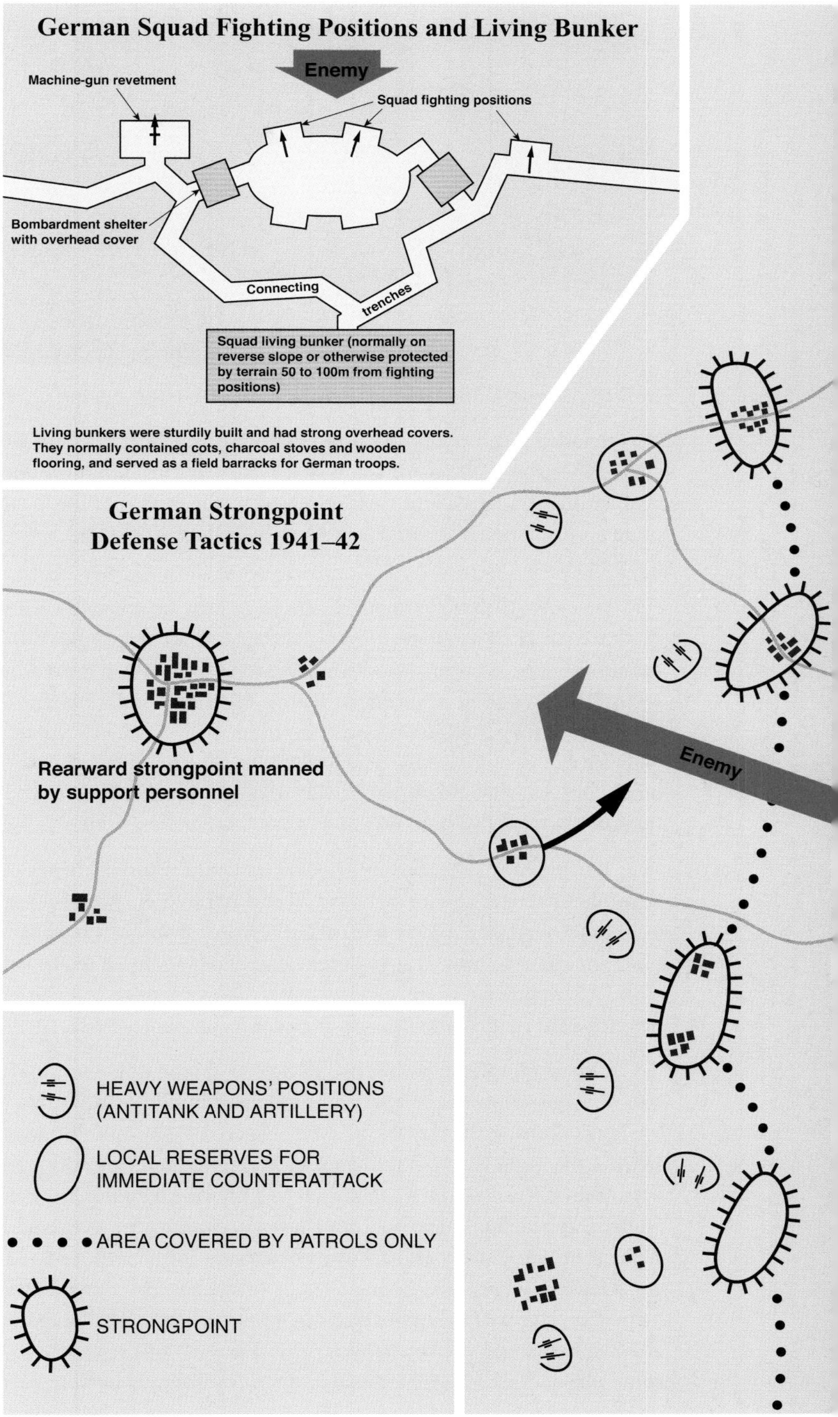

Diagrams and info in this section based on Wray (1986). *U.S. Army*

German Squad Fighting Positions and Living Bunker

Enemy

Machine-gun revetment

Squad fighting positions

Bombardment shelter with overhead cover

Connecting trenches

Squad living bunker (normally on reverse slope or otherwise protected by terrain 50 to 100m from fighting positions)

Living bunkers were sturdily built and had strong overhead covers. They normally contained cots, charcoal stoves and wooden flooring, and served as a field barracks for German troops.

German Strongpoint Defense Tactics 1941–42

Rearward strongpoint manned by support personnel

Enemy

HEAVY WEAPONS' POSITIONS (ANTITANK AND ARTILLERY)

LOCAL RESERVES FOR IMMEDIATE COUNTERATTACK

● ● ● ● AREA COVERED BY PATROLS ONLY

STRONGPOINT

The weapons on shoulders to the left are Czech ZB-53 7.9mm heavy machine guns designated MG 37(t). Both sides were ruthless when it came to scorched earth tactics, although the Soviets were more likely to resettle the inhabitants than leave them homeless. *NAC*

In Defense and Withdrawal: 12. Infanterie-Division during Operation *Bagration*

This detailed examination of a unit's defense and retreat at the start of Operation *Bagration* exemplifies the last year of the war for the German infantryman as they dug in, defended against major attacks, and then retreated to the next suitable location—if they were allowed to do so. Too often, they were told to fight and die in place or were overrun by the strength of the Red Army.

In early 1944 12. Infanterie-Division was attached to XXXIX. Panzerkorps, part of 4. Armee, east of Mogilev. Heavy fighting in March and April left the German formations exhausted. The division took over defense of the River Pronja bend—a 32-kilometer-wide sector that required all three infantry regiments and Fusilier-Bataillon 12 (hitherto the reconnaissance battalion) to be employed in the forward line. Apart from the field replacement battalion, operational only to a limited extent, the division had no reserves. Commanding officer of I./Fusilier-Regiment 27 was Major Heinz-Georg Lemm. His battalion sector, on the right flank of the division, was more than 4 kilometers wide.

During May 1944 the three fusilier companies and the heavy company were brought back to combat strength again—between 70 and 100 soldiers per company. In June the battalion had a strength of approximately 430 men. For combat support purposes it was allocated a platoon of 7.5cm infantry guns. Due to the extremely wide combat sector, only one artillery battalion— with 12.5cm howitzers and a heavy battery with 15cm guns—was able to bring its firepower to bear forward of the battalion's positions. All companies had an artillery FOO.

The terrain the battalion had to defend sloped down to the river. On the right there was flat, wet grassland where it was impossible to build positions, but which was also unsuitable for tanks. During the day it could be observed easily and dominated with machine-gun fire. During the night the 1.5-kilometer-wide gap to the neighboring unit was covered by infantry patrols. In the centre and up to the left neighboring battalion the Pronja, a river of 15–25-meter width, was a tank obstacle but only a few places along the river could be observed, so that every night standing patrols and forward observers from both sides advanced to spot or disturb construction work for crossing sites or obstacles. The most forward-placed German trench formed a system of firing positions and machine-gun pits linked by connecting trenches and all weapons could deliver flanking fire. Forward of the positions there were mines and, in some places, barbed-wire entanglements. The soldiers lived in earth bunkers usually located on reverse slopes. These bunkers had a capacity of up to 10 soldiers and during enemy attacks formed the backbone for three to five fighting positions. Based on the analysis of earlier Soviet offensive operations, Lemm prepared a second trench and fighting positions 400–600 meters behind the most forward positions, as far as possible on reverse slopes, and, in addition, covered connecting trenches between the first and second positions.

The eight weeks of hard work it took to create these secondary positions was proved worthwhile when almost all the first position's trenches and bunkers were destroyed by several hours' artillery and mortar fire at the start of the Soviet attack on June 22 and 23. The battalion, however, suffered few casualties as it had withdrawn—except for some observers—to the second position just before the Russian attack began. Only when Soviet infantry and tanks attacked across the river did the battalion reoccupy the forward positions.

Since Lemm's sector was regarded as being relatively tank-safe, he realized he'd be unlikely to get support from the 10 assault guns recently supplied to the division. He created his own reserve for counterattacks and to protect his open right flank: two understrength platoons led by the commander of the 4. (heavy weapons) Kompanie, whose HMGs and mortars were positioned over the entire width of the battalion's area of defense.

On June 21, the Russian artillery delivered heavy harassing fire, and their scout parties and combat patrols tried to cross the river. Around 12:00 on the 22nd the Soviets attacked and were repulsed. General Martinek's foresight paid off in getting the artillery batteries to register numerous targets in the forward area and to open fire only when the enemy had been located and identified at one of the target points; by so doing, he saved ammunition. The flanking machine-gun positions also turned out to be very useful.

Mortars played an important defensive role and were used frequently to disrupt Soviet attacks. The German standard early war infantry mortar was the 5cm leGrW 36. It was trigger-fired and man-portable in two parts but had no sighting system other than the Mk 1 eyeball. It was soon discarded (an Eigener sketch). *RCT*

The division expected further Russian attacks the next day, so Lemm withdrew the main body of the battalion to the second-line positions again. All night the Russians illuminated the battlefield with searchlights and flares. At 04:00 a rolling barrage moved back and forth across the battalion's forward positions and the positions of the heavy weapons. After almost three hours of uninterrupted fire, all the minefields and barbed-wire entanglements, all communication links and most of the fighting positions of the first-line trench had been destroyed by the attacking Russian infantry. With some 40 casualties the battalion's losses were high but would have been higher without the second-line position. The Soviets had succeeded in preparing three crossing sites and six to eight tanks were on the German side in the wet meadows, stuck but firing. The German low combat strength turned out to be an advantage when they reoccupied the first-line trench and, despite the

The 5cm mortar was superseded by the rifle grenade—here about to be fired once the target has been identified. *NAC*

destruction, found enough good positions. The first enemy attacks broke down about 200 meters in front of the German position. Further attacks in the early afternoon were also repelled after a local penetration at the 1. Kompanie position was eliminated by the reserve company and the battalion HQ under Lemm's command. During the night there was repeated surprise fire from the enemy artillery and once again Lemm withdrew to the second trench which the Soviets did not seem to have recognized despite the illumination of the battlefield.

On the morning of the 24th there was more heavy artillery fire, along with Russian aircraft attacks. More infantry attacks followed, this time without tank support—it seemed the wet meadows had deterred the Russians. The battalion succeeded in holding the forward line, but casualties were rising, and ammunition was running low. Contact with the unit on the right was lost; a patrol sent to reestablish contact met Soviet tanks advancing to the east.

Around 17:30 the regimental CP transmitted that it was being attacked from the north and that the regiment commander, Oberstleutnant Gerhard Engel, had been wounded. By 20:00 the battlefield was profoundly silent, but Lemm's regiment could hear tank fire behind. As the Germans didn't have any tanks, they had to be Russian. Around 21:30—it was getting dark—Lemm decided the battalion should quit its position; all its neighbors had lost their positions. The 9. Kompanie of the left battalion had lost contact with its own unit and so attached to Lemm's. He established a covering force and gave the order to march westwards at 22:00, arranging his troops in the form of an inverted wedge. The covering force followed at an interval of half an hour. The battalion moved past the division's evacuated artillery positions and service support facilities. The area was littered with vehicles and guns which seemed to have been destroyed by air attacks. Several stragglers, wire patrols of a signal unit, motorcycle messengers and even an artillery supply vehicle joined the retreating unit which moved on byroads and avoided the so-called *Rollbahn*, the division's makeshift main supply route. There were lots of Soviet aircraft, but they were dropping their flares to the west.

At dawn Lemm made radio contact with Fusilier-Regiment 27's other battalion that was in contact with the regimental command post some 6 kilometers away. Both battalions moved into positions forward of the Resta River. At noon, they were attacked by 15 Russian tanks with mounted infantry. Although they had no antitank weapons, the battalion repelled this and another enemy attack, destroying two enemy tanks. After three days without sleep and the night march, during which the fusiliers had to carry all weapons, radio sets, and ammunition, the soldiers were exhausted. That evening, the division was ordered to withdraw to a protective position on the far bank of the Dnieper. Lemm's battalion, acting as the division's rear covering force, stayed where it was overnight, thus allowing half the fusiliers to get some sleep for two or three hours before the retreat continued.

Tanks and Infantry

As the war progressed, the dispersing of tanks and assault guns to forward units for local counterattack became an increasingly contentious doctrinal issue. What the infantry commanders wanted was tanks in company or platoon strength to support their own tactical reserves. Panzers should—the infantry felt—be placed under local infantry commanders much as the *Sturmgeschütze* were. Furthermore, in exceptional cases (as it was for the hard-pressed 336. Infanterie-Division on the Chir River in December 1942), German infantrymen also wanted some tanks placed at their disposal to act as mobile antitank guns in support of their static positions. As expected, German panzer officers vigorously denounced all these ideas, preferring a freer role.

What they specifically wanted was the free rein to concentrate armor in large enough quantities to allow its use against Soviet breakthroughs as *Truppenführung* suggested:

> Tanks are employed offensively. They are a decisive reserve in the hands of the commander, especially suitable for general counterattack [*Gegenangriff*] or for the engagement of hostile tanks … Ordinarily their assembly position is far to the rear out of effective hostile artillery range … In general, tanks are employed on orders of the higher commander, who controls the time and objective of the attack and the cooperation of other arms.

However, the infantrymen were not impressed by the occasional successes of concentrated armor in annihilating Russian breakthrough forces. These victorious panzer battles—such as those of Balck's 11. Panzer-Division on the Chir River in December 1942—too often came only after the forward infantry had been all but wiped out.

The Panzer Training School in Wünsdorf set out its views in the February 1943 *Instructional Pamphlet on Cooperation Between Panzers and Infantry in the Defense*. It suggested the following principles for employing tanks in the defense (although the pamphlet wasn't circulated as German Army doctrine):

Two StuG IIIs providing cover and fire support during the advance through Kharkov in 1941. (An Eigener sketch.) *RCT*

- Tanks should only be employed in counterattacks and never as part of a static defense;
- Tanks should be held far enough behind the front so that they could be used against enemy penetrations across a wide sector;
- Tanks should never be committed piecemeal to the defense but should always be employed en masse;
- "En masse" meant at least a tank battalion—around 40 tanks—with infantry support.

In reality, tanks couldn't work on their own. They needed infantry support. Balck's brilliant defense along the Chir River was as much a success of his motorized infantry—Panzergrenadier-Regimenten 110 and 111—as it was of his tanks. Massing quantities of armor was a nice idea but by 1943 German tank strength was not what it was. As the war wore on, battalions could rarely muster half of their TO&E strength. Compromise and flexibility became more important than doctrine.

Infantry–Tank Cooperation

This was a skill that was hard learned. Panzer tactics were often more concerned with counterattacks in force than helping the infantry. The *Sturmgeschütz* (StuG) was designed to cooperate with infantry although, once a suitable gun had been introduced, its antitank use increased as the war went on. Indeed, it's thought to have killed more enemy tanks than any other German AFV. More, with variations, were produced than any other fully tracked armored vehicle. In 1942 a new outline of the employment of StuGs was produced. It suggested:

- the StuG's primary function was infantry support, especially to be used against strongpoints. This cooperation was emphasized—particularly when it came to targets;
- infantry protection was always necessary because of its vulnerability (particularly weak armor on sides and top). It was best used in units rather than piecemeal so they could self-support;
- the *Sturmgeschütz-Bataillon* came under artillery control. Its TOE had an HQ and three gun batteries (each had seven StuGs, a battery commander's vehicle, and three platoons of two guns). Local control of the StuGs was by the infantry unit they were supporting;
- in defense, the StuGs were best used offensively, in counterattacks.

Infantry follow closely behind their supporting StuG IIIs. *SF collection*

Tank Hunting

In 1985 Gen Ferdinand Maria von Senger und Etterlin said:

> Close combat against tanks required well-trained, courageous soldiers with good nerves because they usually had to spring at the tank while their fellow soldiers supported them with rifle fire on the vision blocks of the tanks or with smoke grenades. Although this close combat method against tanks involved considerable risk, the soldiers of my battalion killed more than 14 Russian tanks in this way during the Soviet offensive. Snipers were given the task of firing on the tank commander thus forcing the crew to close the hatches, because, with the hatches closed, visibility for the Russian driver was very bad. Each squad of the fusiliers had a tank-killer team consisting of two soldiers, with one soldier having to cover the other. In their fight against tanks our soldiers were particularly thankful for support by assault guns.

Antitank warfare often ended up being a visceral close-combat affair where steely resolve made the difference. Gerhard Konopka was a man with such resolve. On November 19, 1942, Reichsminister Dr Joseph Goebbels and, behind him, Generalleutnant Paul von Hase, State Commandant of Berlin, receive soldiers who had been fighting in the Rzhev area. Next to von Hase is Oberleutnant Konopka of the Großdeutschland Division who has four tank destruction badges—the *Sonderabzeichen für das Niederkämpfen von Panzerkampfwagen durch Einzelkämpfer*—on his sleeve. By the time this photograph was taken Konopka had been awarded both classes of Iron Cross the Infantry Assault and two wound badges, the *Deutsches Kreuz in Gold* and four tank destruction badges—for knocking out tanks on September 1, 22 and 23 and on October 12, 1942. He would go on to be awarded the *Nahkampfspange in Gold*, a third wound badge (on July 18, 1943), and the *Ritterkreuz. SF collection*

The German 5cm antitank guns, with which Kompanie 14 of each regiment was equipped, were nowhere near powerful enough to face large numbers of attacking tanks. Infantrymen often ended up using close-combat weapons such as antitank mines, block charges and adhering mines like the *Hafthohlladung* (hand-held hollow charge) that had to be attached to a tank to work. The arrival of the Panzerschreck and Panzerfaust made a big difference to the tank busters, as did the arrival—albeit in small numbers—of heavier antitank guns and better armor-piercing ammunition. Here, men of the Großdeutschland Division in Memel carry *Panzerfäuste. Bundesarchiv 146-1995-081-31A*

INFANTERIE GREIFT AN!

Counterattacks

The Germans were known for their doctrine of counterattacking to regain lost ground. *Truppenführung* says:

> Should a portion of the main battle position be lost, we must first strive through fire to annihilate the enemy who has penetrated. Our infantry elements and supporting weapons which are in proximity of the penetration endeavor by immediate local counterattack to hurl back the enemy before he has opportunity to establish himself. These elements can be effectively supported by artillery fire laid in rear of the enemy who has penetrated the position. However, they must not be dependent upon the artillery cooperation.
>
> Should the above measures fail, or should the enemy make a large penetration, the higher commander decides whether a general counterattack will be made to restore the position or whether the main battle position is to be taken up further to the rear. The counterattack, where possible, is to be launched against the hostile flank. The counterattack requires, especially when undertaken by strong forces, thorough preparation. Assembly positions, time, objective, zones, artillery support, employment of tanks and air force units must be controlled by one commander. Too great haste leads to failure … Forces which are to be employed in counterattack against an enemy which breaks into the main battle position must be held well forward.

Sometimes, especially if the enemy was clued up enough to range its artillery correctly, counterattacks could be repulsed bloodily, but German unit combat reports unanimously said that immediate, aggressive counterattacks (*Gegenstoße*)—even when conducted using limited means—were the best way to defeat Russian penetrations. Waiting to prepare a

Above left: MG 34 giving covering fire for the attack: hit hard and consolidate. *RCT*

Left: Keeping low when using cover. There are two categories of cover: from view and from fire. Here an MG team makes the most of cover to keep from view as it moves into position to support an attack (a German Army postcard). *RCT*

more deliberate counterattack (*Gegenangriff*) was less effective. Indeed, the operations officer of the 78. Division, talking about the first winter, stated that "a *Gegenstoß* thrown immediately against an enemy break-in, even if only in squad strength, achieves more than a deliberate counterattack in company or battalion strength on the next day."

Static Positions

A well-finished battle position, as a rule

> embraces a series of mutually supporting defensive areas with obstacles, trenches, and nests of individual arms. The positions are distributed irregularly and strongly in depth and are erected in the sequence of their importance. At particularly important areas strongpoints of different arms should be laid out. The plan of defense should be difficult to recognize both on the ground and from the air. Adjacent sectors must be able to support each other. Too great a striving for flanking support must not invalidate the frontal defense … a sure connection between all sectors must be built up. Obstacles, dummy works, measured points in the terrain in front of the position, the removal of distinctive objects in the position, camouflage, observation posts and communication trenches complete the defensive layout.

A U.S. Army assessment of German positions identifies the various layers: advanced position held by reconnaissance elements 5–7,000 meters in front of the main line of resistance (MLR) (unless the front is stabilized, in which case it is omitted); outposts 2–5,000 meters ahead, protected by artillery; then the battle positions in depth along the MLR.

> Individual strongpoints connected to form an uninterrupted belt. The strongpoints, constructed for all-around defense, and surrounded by barbed-wire obstacles and mine belts, contain one or more heavy weapons supplemented by machine guns, mortars, and riflemen. The

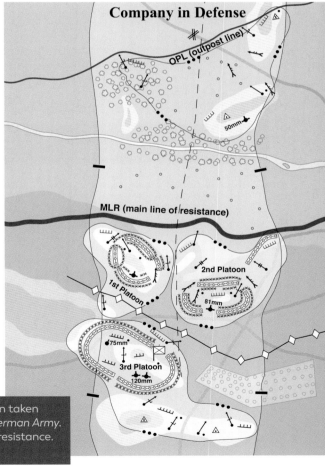

German company in a defensive position taken from the U.S. Army's *Handbook of the German Army*. OPL = outpost line; MLR = main line of resistance. For key see next page. *U.S. Army*

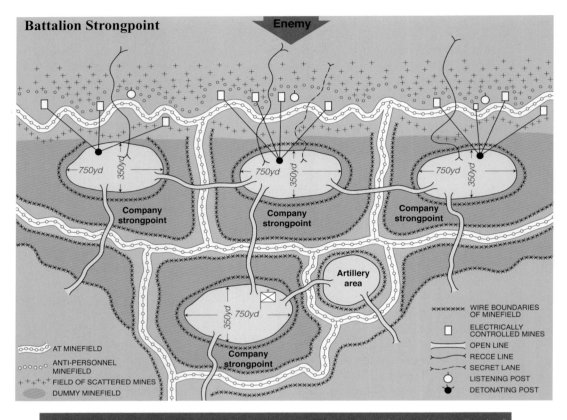

Battalion Strongpoint

Enemy

750yd 350yd

Company strongpoint

750yd 350yd

Company strongpoint

750yd 350yd

Company strongpoint

Artillery area

350yd 750yd

Company strongpoint

AT MINEFIELD

ANTI-PERSONNEL MINEFIELD

+ + + + FIELD OF SCATTERED MINES

DUMMY MINEFIELD

×××××× WIRE BOUNDARIES OF MINEFIELD

ELECTRICALLY CONTROLLED MINES

OPEN LINE

RECCE LINE

SECRET LANE

LISTENING POST

DETONATING POST

Typical layout of a reinforced battalion strongpoint from the U.S. Army's *Handbook of the German Army. U.S. Army*

Dig, dig, and dig: a lifesaving necessity. This soldier is using a folding shovel (*Klappspaten*). NAC

Trench with a bend which prevents an enemy from firing down its full length. The MG assistant has a spare barrel container over his shoulder. The observer has his MP 40 and prepared M24 and EihGr 39 grenades. NAC

smallest strongpoint is occupied by a reinforced squad. Squad strongpoints normally are incorporated into platoon strongpoints, and the latter into company strongpoints, etc … The Germans make the maximum use of reverse slopes in their defensive positions. Forward-slope positions are usually avoided as they are detected too early by the enemy and are likely to be destroyed by massed fire.

[They] stress construction of obstacles and antitank defenses. If possible, they select tank-proof terrain, and natural tank obstacles, such as steep slopes, are improved. Very steep forward slopes are made at least 8 yards deep, while uphill slopes are made 2 to 3 yards high. Originally the Germans constructed antitank ditches well forward of the main line of resistance, but experience taught them that such ditches offered favorable jumping-off positions for hostile infantry and also revealed the location of the main line of resistance. At the present time, therefore, antitank ditches normally are dug in the area between the main line of resistance and the artillery positions. They are built in an uninterrupted line to avoid leaving passages that can be exploited by the enemy.

The Germans learned that dense minefields in front of their positions were an inadequate tank obstacle, because the enemy usually neutralized them by massed artillery fire or by concentrated air bombardment before launching a large-scale attack. Now German minefields normally are laid within the main battle position, and only single mines are dispersed in pattern at wide intervals in front of the main line of resistance. Particular stress is placed on the mining of roads. Routes of withdrawal which have to be left open are prepared for mining, and, if time does not permit placing of actual mines, dummy mines are installed.

40 Grad Kälte, translating to "40 degrees of cold," a watercolor by Obergefreiter Fritz Brauner from *Soldaten in Eis und Schnee (Soldiers in Ice and Snow)*. It shows a 2cm Flak 30 position. Note the wooden-soled, leather, canvas, and felt over boots essential for use in snow. The 2cm or 3.7cm antiaircraft gun was also very successful in ground operations. *RCT*

Making Shelters with Explosives

By early January 1942 German frostbite numbers had risen to an unsustainable rate that made immediate creation of shelters and bunkers essential. There were too few engineers and not enough suitable equipment available. There were, however, lots of explosives and these were used to blast craters in the frozen ground big enough to hold three to five men. Reserves and service troops packed down paths between the craters and to the rear. Any available wood was used to cover the craters. The engineers who prepared the positions suffered numerous frostbite casualties but immediately contributed to reduced frostbite.

Sniping

In the 1930s, the German Army felt that sniping was unique to trench warfare and obsolete in the modern world but that quickly changed. Because of the lack of official equipment initially privately acquired scopes were employed. The first official development was the Zf39 (*Das Zielfernrohr 39 für den Karabiner 98k*). By May 21, 1940, 1,340 calibrated rifles and Zf39 scopes were delivered by Mauser. The Polish campaign led to a call for a scope to help marksmen—as opposed to snipers—and led to the Zf41, the most widely produced of the German optical devices: by May 1943, 87,396 had been delivered and production continued into 1945. The K98k wasn't the only German sniping weapon. Scopes were made for the Gewehr 41, Gewehr 43, Sturmgewehr 44, and top mounts for both models of the Luftwaffe FG 42.

The Waffen-SS was also interested in sniping using any World War I scoped rifles they could find. They also used commercial suppliers like J. P. Sauer & Sohn or Gustloff Werke.

The extreme temperatures of the Russian winter led to problems for snipers. As well as their bolts and actions freezing along with the lubricants, scopes rated for cold weather could not go below −4°C and adjustments could not be made on them.

Below left: The ZF-41 1.5 x had a long eye relief—the distance between eye and optics—making it useless as a sniper scope. However, it could make a good shot into a better one. *Bundesarchiv 101I-455-0013-15*

Below right: Care of weapons and equipment is always important—particularly for snipers. This team is in Romania. The spotter (left) is cleaning his binoculars while the sniper cleans his turret-mounted K98k. Note the chain pull-through bore-cleaner in his left hand, part of the K98k cleaning kit. *SF collection*

Sniper team: spotter and sharpshooter with a turret-mounted K98k. *NAC*

The *Anleitung für die Ausbildung und den Einsatz von Scharfschützen* (Instructions for the training and use of snipers) suggested that snipers be used in attack and defense:

In the attack, the sharpshooter can be given the following tasks:

- Particularly dangerous targets that hinder progress;
- Monitoring the actions of the group or a patrol;
- Taking over the flank protection.

When attacking, the sharpshooter positions himself a little to the side of the group to be able to shoot unhindered.

As a rule, the sniper must select the most dangerous targets or those targets which, if destroyed, will cause the greatest damage to the enemy. Examples of dangerous targets are snipers, observers or operators of heavy weapons. Shooting down guides, dispatchers, ammunition suppliers, tank commanders, etc. hits the enemy hardest.

In defense, the sharpshooter must dominate enemy trenches with his fire. No careless movement of the enemy must escape him. For this reason, the sharpshooter is to be given freedom of movement in the selection of his position in the section of group, platoon, and often also the company. The sharpshooter can, therefore, depending on location and terrain, be in the front line or further back, e.g., take position at a commanding height or in a tree.

In order not to give himself away, the sharpshooter should generally not fire more than three to six shots from a position and often take alternating positions. Continuous observation of the enemy by sharpshooters must be ensured.

If the enemy behaves too cautiously as a result of sharpshooter activity, it is advisable to stop shooting for one or more days in order to induce the enemy to make careless movements again. On bright and sunny days, with snowfall in winter, the opponent tends to be careless about food and drink, so that a good sharpshooter will always find targets.

On sniping teams the instructions suggested:

It is advisable to assign an observer with binoculars to the sniper. Both have to move like hunters and lie in wait. The observer supports the sniper in observing the enemy territory and in watching the gunshots. If the enemy does not offer a target for a long time or if he is also on the lookout, shooters and observers must try to lure the enemy into firing by cunning deceptions, but only if they are performed skillfully and reasonably. Example: the observer appears for a moment in a trench, then reappears again for a short time in order to draw the attention of the opponent. A few minutes later, the observer pushes a helmet or a helmet-like object over the cover, causing the opponent to shoot in most cases. A straw doll can also be used. The more varied the deceptions, the greater the success for the sniper will be.

| Life in the Field

The German Army that invaded the Soviet Union in 1941 was not used to long campaigns. They had beaten the Poles in 35 days; the Netherlands had fallen in eight; Belgium in 18; Norway took 62 days; France six weeks. They didn't expect a long campaign in the east and it came as a shock when the Soviets didn't give way as the others had done. This was a surprise and while the army had thought about a long campaign, it had not believed it would happen. The first casualty was winter clothing in the face of a bitter winter. Supply issues would be a continuous problem, particularly when dependent on the Luftwaffe for help.

It was not just supply problems that plagued the German Army. By the time they reached Moscow, they had lost significant numbers of not just men, but leaders.

By the end of September, the Ostheer, while inflicting three to four million casualties on the enemy, had suffered half a million in so doing itself. This loss represented 30 division equivalents, and a like strength of officers and NCOs to man 37 from 117 divisions; leadership losses, representing probably one-third of the total, were key.

They hadn't beaten the Soviets whose winter campaign came as a complete shock to soldiers who were used to winning. And as the victories became fewer, so shock turned to fatalism. Fresh food became difficult to procure; hardships increased. But remarkably, the German soldiers showed toughness and perseverance in adversity. Even as the bombing campaign over Germany brought death to their wives and loved ones, even as the casualties mounted in their own ranks, the German infantryman fought tenaciously, even in the mud and cold, even when the battle had become a fight for German existence. As Goebbels wrote on November 15, 1942, in *Das Reich* newspaper, "We have thrown our whole national existence into the balance. There is no turning back now."

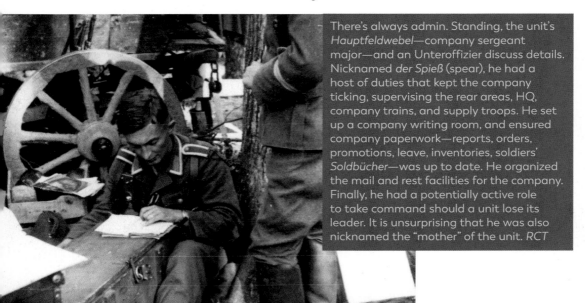

There's always admin. Standing, the unit's *Hauptfeldwebel*—company sergeant major—and an Unteroffizier discuss details. Nicknamed *der Spieß* (spear), he had a host of duties that kept the company ticking, supervising the rear areas, HQ, company trains, and supply troops. He set up a company writing room, and ensured company paperwork—reports, orders, promotions, leave, inventories, soldiers' *Soldbücher*—was up to date. He organized the mail and rest facilities for the company. Finally, he had a potentially active role to take command should a unit lose its leader. It is unsurprising that he was also nicknamed the "mother" of the unit. *RCT*

Behind the lines security—here documents are being scrutinized. The man in the background is wearing Russian felt boots—not good in wet weather but for Russian winters indispensable. The best type was unquestionably the Russian pure felt boot (the *valinki*) although it was suitable only during the real frost period. The weapon in the background is an MG 34 with AA sight. It is on an extended AA tripod. Its boxed ammunition is hung on it for stability. *NAC*

This chapter, primarily pictorial, looks at the life of the Landser in the field and behind the lines. It was behind the front line that the SS-Einsatzgruppen and death squads carried out their vile duties. They may have concentrated on exterminating Jews, but Soviet POWs and civilians were also likely to be in the firing line. There is plenty of evidence that many German infantrymen aided and abetted the SS. It wasn't a place of safety for the soldiers either. While they might not have had a war-winning importance, partisan actions did much to ensure that the Germans did not feel completely safe in the territory they had conquered.

SS-Einsatzgruppen death squad. *SF collection*

The sign behind the Feldgendarmerie motorcycle combo tells of the danger of partisans in the area. Single vehicles should stop until they can travel in a convoy. *SF collection*

As with all armies there was a great emphasis on bodily hygiene and being able to change clothing—always a morale booster. The white stripes on the socks indicate size; the more stripes (three) the bigger the socks. *SF collection*

Hygiene also included regular haircuts whenever the opportunity arose. *SF collection*

Entertainment: cards and board games were a good opportunity to forget reality. Note the black cat, even better! *SF collection*

Sawing and chopping wood kept one warm. The second man on the left could be a Hiwi (*Hilfswilliger*) or auxiliary volunteer from the local community. *RCT*

Card school in a railway carriage. *RCT*

Firewood was always important when preparing food and, as the sign indicates, the *Küche* (kitchen) is close by. *RCT*

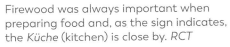

115

Hot food for the frontline. The *Essenträger* was a large aluminum double-skinned container, with hot water between its metal walls, allowing hot food to be carried from the field kitchen to the troops. Needless to say, this could be a perilous journey. The men taking food to the front did what they could, but distance and danger didn't help. The food was often cold. *SF collection; SF*

Below: "Two prisoners taken!" As with all soldiers, the German Army made good use of available foodstuffs. *RCT*

— 2 GEFANGENE GEMACHT!

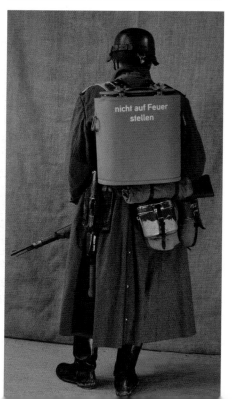

Sometimes doled out from the back of trucks, hot food usually came from the *Feldküche* (field kitchen), nicknamed the *Gulaschkanone* ("goulash cannon," cannon from the chimney). These came in two main forms, the *große Feldküche*—large field kitchen—(Hf 11/13) that could feed 225 and had a *Vorderwagen* limber, and the *kleine Feldküche*—small field kitchen—(Hf 12/14) that fed 125. Initially, the Hf 11 had two kettles, a big one for soup and a smaller for coffee; in 1943, an improved version (Hf 13) included another firebox for meat roasting/stewing, replacing storage areas. **Top left** is the motorized field kitchen of Infanterie-Regiment 15, 291. Infanterie-Division. The division was destroyed in the fighting at Stalingrad. *NARA; RCT (both)*

Feeding the army was as important as giving it arms and ammunition. As with all armies, the Germans had thought carefully about what was needed. The rations were divided into four classes.

- I for combat troops either in the line or recuperating and for those troops deployed in the far north (in northern Norway and Finland). Around 1,700g.
- II for troops in rear areas, the army of occupation and communication troops. Around 1,650g.
- III for garrison units in Germany. Just over 1,600g.
- IV for auxiliary personnel, office workers and nurses in Germany. About 1,480g.

In 1939 the daily per soldier ration was:

750g bread or 500g biscuits
250g meat or 200g bacon or 200g canned meat
100g rice/barley/semolina
200g fresh or 100g canned or 60g dried vegetables
50g fat
40g jam
15g salt
80g sugar
coffee, tea, spirits if available
2 cigars, 5 cigarettes
Total calories: around 4,500

This wasn't given to the soldier direct but to the field kitchen. In the field, food was supplemented locally either through purchase or often by requisition. Soldiers in the field were supposed to get two hot meals a day from the field kitchens staffed by the *Feldkochunteroffizier* (field cooking NCO) and the *Küchenbullen* (his assistants). Lunch amounted to half of the *Portionsatz*—daily ration quantity—the evening meal to a third, and

Units ate together but in the front lines it was from mess cans. *NAC*

Behind the lines: a very relaxed meal among the washing lines. *RCT*

the next morning's breakfast to one-sixth. As well as the hot food soldiers received a daily bread ration with cheese, ham and jam for breakfast and iron or half-iron rations (*eiserne Portionen* or *halb-eiserne Portionen*) as necessary.

German Winter Warfare discusses cold weather food:

> In extremely cold weather, the following rations are especially suitable for the field kitchen: frozen and canned meat; hard salami; bacon; smoked meat; fresh vegetables, including beans and peas; spaghetti; macaroni; noodles; frozen potatoes; and frozen vegetables. Food which has a high water content should not be taken along.
>
> Hot drinks should be issued. If the soldier cannot be fed from the field kitchen, he should be issued the following provisions:
>
> (1) Bread ready for consumption and with some sort of spread on it. The men should wrap it in paper if possible and carry it in their pockets to protect it against the cold; (2) Cracked wheat bread; (3) Dried and baked fruits; (4) Candies; (5) Chocolates.

The range of ration types were:

- March rations (*Marschverpflegung*) for units out of range of a field kitchen. Not issued for more than three or four days—total weight about 1kg (2.2lb) split into 700g of bread, 200g of cold meat or cheese, 60g spreads, 9g of coffee (or 4g of tea), 10g of sugar, and six cigarettes.
- Iron rations (*eiserne Portionen*[1]) for units on missions lasting for at least two days— around 650g of food: 250–300g biscuits (*Zwieback*, *Hartkeks*, or *Knäckebrot*), 200g cold meat (*Fleischkonserve*), 150g preserved vegetables (*Gemüse*) or 150g of canned soup or a pack of *Erbswurst* (pea and sausage) soup concentrate, 25g coffee (*Kaffee-Ersatz*) and 25g salt (*Salz*).
- Iron half-rations (*halb-eiserne Portionen*) were reduced rations only to be eaten on CO's orders or in an emergency (although this was hard to enforce)— about 0.5kg (1lb) of *Zwieback* (hard biscuits) and a tin of preserved meat (200g). These were carried in knapsacks or haversacks.
- Towards the end of the war the Germans tried to emulate the U.S. Army's K rations by producing the *Großkampfpäcken* (combat package) and *Nahkampfpäcken* (close combat package) for troops in combat. Contents varied but included chocolate bars,

---

1   *Portion* (pl *-en*) = rations for humans; *Ration* (pl *-en*) = fodder for horses

fruit bars, sweets, cigarettes, and possibly biscuits. The most popular item was "*Scho-ka-kola*" (a diminutive of *Schokolade, Kaffee, Kolanuß*) which was a performance-enhancing energy chocolate.

One key responsibility of veterinary officers was the supervision of food supplies from animal origins:

> Very frequently units stole cattle and slaughtered it themselves. The failure to examine the meat and a disregard of repeated instructions to the effect that the meat should be served only in small pieces and thoroughly cooked, resulted in numerous fatalities. Motorized units were particularly handicapped since they were often unable to obtain a veterinary officer to inspect their meat. For this and other reasons, as the war went on, individual veterinary officers accompanied motorized and armored divisions insofar as they could be made available. … Trichinosis … was very common among their swine. Entire units became ill and were out of action for several months after consuming trichinous meat. The pork

Mates. All for one and one for all creates a bond unique to those who have served in the military—for many a life-long bond. It was this camaraderie that helped keep German units together even under the direst of circumstances. In the end, why did they fight on when loss seemed inevitable? Partly, it is true, because of the threats and the executions—but mainly because they didn't want to let their mates down. *RCT*

Eager anticipation of news from home. Here, a signaler (note sleeve lightning bolt). *RCT*

Writing home in conditions that prove fighting in the Soviet Union wasn't just mud and snow. *RCT*

Mail received was a connection with home and family and an essential morale booster. Sadly, there would not always be a recipient. As with all military units, if a dead man's parcel contained usable items, they would be shared by his mates. If the opportunity arose his officer would respond to the letters to advise the family of the death before official sources. *RCT*

Winter quarters allowed a wooden construction and heating. *RCT*

The *Hauszelt* could fit 16—snugly! Note the helmets over the tent poles (Villa Wien/Vienna and Praha/Prague). *RCT*

tapeworm, a parasite now very rare in Germany, was frequently present in Russian pigs and, when the meat was not properly inspected, its presence was overlooked by butchers. This resulted in a very considerable rise in the number of tapeworms among the personnel of units affected and, while it is not a serious infection in an individual frequently results in a serious case of cysticercosis.

The 16-man tent made by buttoning together shelter halves, known as a "house tent" (*Hauszelt*), was suitable for use as an emergency winter tent because a warming fire or tent stove could be installed in it. It covered an area of about 25 square meters and was about 3 meters high. It afforded shelter for at least 16 men. If the shelter halves were sewed together, the tent could be erected more rapidly and would provide a greater degree of warmth and protection against the wind.

Winter quarters: shelter provided a semblance of normality and allowed clothes to be mended and decent sleeping accommodation. German instructions were detailed about hygiene:

The sooner you fight vermin, the easier it will be to destroy them. Fix regular hours for delousing. Body lice usually are found in pleats and seams of clothing, bedding, and equipment. During inspection special attention should be paid to these hidden places.

Lice may be eradicated by washing clothing with a cresol-soap solution or with kerosene, and then pressing the garments with a hot iron. Regular use should be made of louse powder. If clothes are too heavily infested with lice, they should be treated in delousing stations by means of dry heat or steam, or, in the case of underclothing, by boiling.

Accommodation with a stove for heating and cooking was a great treasure in wintertime (a Brauner watercolor). *RCT*

The map shows the Black and Caspian seas, Ukraine and the Caucasus so it's likely this image is around the 1942 *Fall Blau* period. *RCT*

If bedbugs appear in great numbers, the quarters should be fumigated with gas. For this purpose, the men must move temporarily to other quarters, but only after having cleaned their bodies thoroughly and deloused their clothes. When returning to their original quarters, the men must observe the precautionary measures laid down by the fumigators.

Death, Remembrance, and POWs

The casualties on the Eastern Front dwarfed those inflicted by the Western Allies, as these figures (dead, missing, or disabled) show. Glantz's figures:

Period	Number	Percentage in east
09.39–1.09.42	922,000	Over 90%
1.09.42–20.11.43	2,077,000	Over 90%
20.11.43–06.44	1,500,000 est.	80%
06–11.44	1,457,000	62%
30.12.44–30.04.45	2,000,000	67%
Total losses to 30.04.45	11,135,500	
	3,888,000 dead	
	3,035,700 captured	
Total Wehrmacht losses	13,488,000	80% (10,758,000)

R. Overmans' figures:

Total During Year	Total Dead
1941	302,000
1942	507,000
1943	701,000
1944	1,233,000
Total 1941–44	2,742,000
Final Battles in Germany	1,230,045

Soviet sources reported that in 1945 the German Army lost more than a million men on the Eastern Front alone. Figures do not include POW deaths of 363,000 in Soviet captivity; these losses were listed separately by Overmans.

Troops say goodbye to fallen comrades—note the ammo boxes, MG 34, and folded Lafette tripods. Heavy—at 20kg—the tripods had pads to allow them to be more comfortably carried. *RCT*

Christliches Andenken

an unseren lieben, unvergeßlichen
Sohn und Bruder

Franz Söllhammer

Pionier in einem Grenadier-Regiment
Traunersohn von Schalchen

der am 3. Dezember 1943 bei den schweren
Abwehrkämpfen um Tscherkassy (Rußland)
im 19. Lebensjahre für seine liebe Heimat
den Heldentod-starb.

Left: Death cards were produced throughout the war for the family, often by friends and comrades. Here, Franz Söllhammer—in *Fraktur*, German Gothic script—was a *Pionier* (engineer) in a grenadier regiment and died on December 3, 1943, in heavy defensive battles in the northwest Caucasus "for his beloved homeland." *RCT*

Above: Looking after the dead, burying them, and marking their graves is important, particularly to soldiers in far-off lands. *NARA*

Below: Hitlerjugend were called to defend Germany in the last weeks of the war. *SF collection*

Some 91,000 German soldiers surrendered when Stalingrad fell. *SF collection*

| Conclusion

In 1939–42 German infantrymen were the best trained and most efficient soldiers in the Western world. Their victories in Europe optimized the use of new technology and old skillsets to overpower their enemies in a series of lightning thrusts. Spearheaded by airborne special forces and armor, fully supported by a rampant air arm, quite simply they blew away the opposition and made fools of the Allies who had defeated an older generation of Germans so comprehensively in 1918.

The most significant element of their superiority wasn't their tanks and dive-bombers, much as both helped, but their incisive leadership—and not just by the senior officers. Their mission-led approach to battlefield tactics and initiative, stemming from the Prussian *Auftragstaktik*, meant that intent was more important than specifics when it came to giving orders. If the intent was clear, subordinates had flexibility to achieve the goal. Responsibility allied with adaptability meant that the job often got done without the need for the sort of hands-on control visible in other armies of the period, whose speed of reaction was never faster than the Germans' speed of decisive action.

Highly motivated by a militarized regime, fueled by their racial and political policies, burning with the supposed injustice of the Treaty of Versailles and of having being stabbed in the back in 1918, wave after wave of German youth went if not happily to war then at least into active service convinced of the need to fight the "Jewish-Bolshevik" enemy to the east, whose lands and raw materials were so necessary for the expansion of their race.

They didn't see what we can see with hindsight: that the Nazi regime was a mishmash of political incompetence and power struggles, that were ill-equipped to sustain a long-term war; that—like Rome before it—the Nazis needed the wealth and the manpower of the nations they conquered to sustain their war effort; and that Nazism's genocidal aims would compromise the very integrity of the German Army to make the way it dealt with civilians and POWs indistinguishable from that of the SS-Einsatzgruppen and Nazi death squads that followed in the army's wake.

Convinced of their inevitable—and speedy—victory, they attacked the Soviet Union, their erstwhile ally, and soon their success could be numbered in hundreds of thousands of enemy killed and captured along with huge swathes of the country. Soon the front line extended for 2,000 miles from Murmansk to the Caucasus. Behind it was an enormous hinterland, much of it difficult swampy or forested terrain that proved ideal for partisans and freedom fighters. And the German Army was just too small, its own casualties too large and the enemy too unbowed for final victory to arrive. They could never deal the Soviets the final killer punch and as they looked over the few kilometers between the apogee of their success and the onion domes of Moscow, the German infantrymen could not have foreseen the torment that lay ahead.

Slowly, their enemy—whose resolve had been obvious even in the first days of *Barbarossa*—held the Germans and then started to push them back. The Landsers learned what retreat looked like. They lost their incisive leaders as their Führer took over supreme control of the battle and the army generals proved too weak to stop him. *Auftragstaktik* gave way to *Befehlstaktik*: micro-managed direct orders that led to standing fast, with no retreat and no flexibility. There were small losses at first but then, as their opponents improved their own leadership abilities and as the productive might of the Western democracies provided Lend-Lease support, the inevitable happened. Operation *Bagration* in summer 1944 saw the Red Army reach Poland and the Carpathians. Desperate defense couldn't stop the Baltic states falling, a giant pocket forming in Courland, and the liberation of the Balkans and Eastern Europe. The next offensive in January 1945 took the Red Army to the Oder and the borders of Germany itself, by which time German arrogant expectation of victory had been replaced by cynicism and despair.

Our knowledge of the Eastern Front battles for many years was tinged by the politics of the Cold War. Desperate to shore up European defenses against the perceived "Red menace," a powerful Germany was an essential bulwark of NATO's central front which was where the next war was anticipated—and it wasn't "if" that war happened, it was "when." Seemingly overnight the West's recent enemies became part of the solution. The Wehrmacht's deep complicity in the Holocaust and the aggressive and ruthless handling of Soviet civilians and POWs was quietly forgotten as German generals returned to the foreground to bolster the rebirth of the German armed forces. The whitewashing of the army was never quite replicated for the actions of the Waffen-SS, but the many papers and biographies of the 1950s allowed much of the German Army to cover up its actions in the east by pointing at Soviet excesses in victory. It didn't take long before a new myth emerged: that the German Army—with its brilliant leadership, excellent weapons, and brave soldiers fighting against the ravening hordes of communist butchers—was only defeated by weight of numbers and the dead, palsied hand of a jumped-up corporal at the helm. The generals played to the galleries, emphasizing their own prowess, bigging-up the importance of Western generals and the common heritage that placed a revitalized Germany in the front line against the Reds.

It's only in recent years, with the opening of Soviet archives, that historians have taken tentative steps towards a more rounded view of the Eastern Front. This recognizes the remarkable skills of the German infantryman who fought there in difficult—almost impossible—circumstances: terrain and weather were big factors; so too were ineffective industry and logistics. Poor command and leadership played a significant part, as did their opponents' numbers, but that's only part of the story. The determination and bravery of the Soviet citizens defending their homeland; the way the Soviet Army learned to win; the effectiveness of Soviet deception operations; the inventiveness that led to the T-34 and Katyusha—all these show it was not just about numbers. Indeed, they also show that the German defense in the east—a horse-drawn army whose recruits got steadily younger and less well trained—was, perhaps, even more remarkable than has been thought.

The vast size of the Eastern Front—from the Arctic to the Black Sea—stretched German transport and communications to breaking point. Sketch from Ernst Eigener's *Skizzen aus dem Ostfeldzug* (*Sketches from the Eastern Campaign*). RCT

| Further Reading

Baird, Jay W.: "The Myth of Stalingrad," *Journal of Contemporary History* 4, No. 3 (1969 accessed at http://www.jstor.org/stable/259739).

Baxter, Ian: *Kursk 1943: Last German Offensive in the East*; Casemate Publishers, 2020.

Beraud, Yves: *German Mountain Troops 1939–42*; Casemate Publishers, 2020.

Beraud, Yves: *German Mountain Troops 1942–45*; Casemate Publishers, 2021.

Buffetaut, Yves: *From Moscow to Stalingrad: The Eastern Front, 1941–1942*; Casemate Publishers, 2018.

Buffetaut, Yves: *The 2nd SS Panzer Division Das Reich*; Casemate Publishers, 2018.

Brunhaver, John Steven: "Lifeline from the Sky"; thesis; Air University Press, 1996.

Chew, Dr. Allen F.: *Leavenworth Papers No. 5 Fighting the Russians in Winter*; Combat Studies Institute, 1981.

CMH Pub 104-14-1 *German Defense Tactics Against Russian Breakthroughs*; CMH, 1984.

DA PAM 20-234 *Operations of Encircled Forces: German Experiences in Russia*; Washington, D.C., 1952.

DA PAM 20-244 *The Soviet Partisan Movement 1941–1944*; Edgar M. Howell, Washington, D.C., 1956.

DA PAM 20-269 *Small Unit Actions During the German Campaign in Russia*; Washington, D.C., 1953.

Davis, Brian L.: *German Army Uniforms and Insignia 1933–1945*; Brockhampton Press, 1992.

Glantz, D. et al.: *Transcript of Proceedings, Art of War Symposium: From the Don to the Dnepr: Soviet Offensive Operations—December 1942–August 1943*; Center for Land Warfare, U.S. Army War College, 1984.

Glantz, D. et al.: *Transcript of Proceedings, Art of War Symposium: From the Dnepr to the Vistula: Soviet Offensive Operations—November 1943–August 1944*; Center for Land Warfare, U.S. Army War College, 1985.

Glantz, D. et al.: *Transcript of Proceedings, Art of War Symposium: From the Vistula to the Oder: Soviet offensive operations—October 1944–March 1945*; Center for Land Warfare, U.S. Army War College, 1986.

Kershaw, Robert: *War Without Garlands*; Ian Allan Ltd, 2000.

Liedtke, Gregory: *Wolverhampton Military Studies No. 21 Enduring the Whirlwind*; Helion & Company, 2016.

Mueller, Richard: *The German Air War in Russia*; Nautical & Aviation Pub. Co. of America, 1992.

Müller-Hillebrand, Generalmajor Burkhart: *Horses in the German Army 1941–1945*; Historical Division, USAREUR, 1951.

Nafziger, George F.: *The German Order of Battle: Infantry in World War II*; Greenhill Books, 2000.

Ruffner, Kevin Conley and Volstad, Ron: *Men at Arms 229 Luftwaffe Field Divisions 1941–45*; Osprey, 1990.

Special Series, *No. 8 German Tactical Doctrine*; Military Intelligence Service, 1942.

Special Series, *No. 9 The German Squad in Combat*; Military Intelligence Service, 1943.

Thomas, Dr Nigel and Shumate, Johnny: *Elite 218 World War II German Motorized Infantry & Grenadiers*; Osprey, 2017.

Tiquet, Pierre: *The 3rd SS Panzer Regiment: 3rd SS Panzer Division Totenkopf*; Casemate Publishers, 2020.

Westwood, David & Sharp, Elizabeth: *Warrior 93 German Infantryman (3) Eastern Front 1943–45*; Osprey, 2002.

Wray, Maj Timothy A.: *Standing Fast: German Defensive Doctrine on the Russian Front During World War II*; Research Survey No. 5, CSI, 1986.

Ziemke, Earl F.: *Army Historical Series Stalingrad to Berlin*; CMH, 1968.

| Index